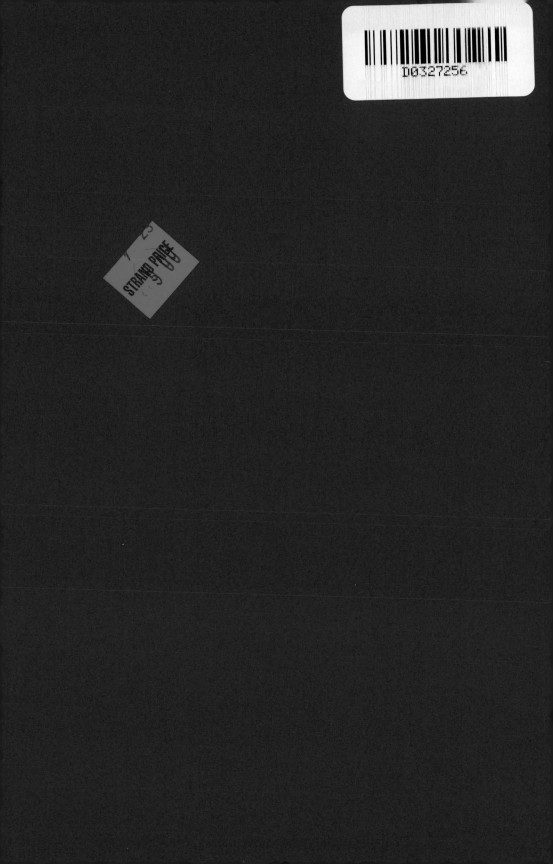

All Falling Faiths

All Falling Faiths

Reflections on the Promise and Failure of the 1960s

J. HARVIE WILKINSON III

Encounter Books
New York · London

First American edition published in 2017 by Encounter Books, an activity of Encounter for Culture and Education, Inc., a nonprofit, tax-exempt corporation. Encounter Books website address: www.encounterbooks.com

Manufactured in the United States and printed on acid-free paper. The paper used in this publication meets the minimum requirements of ANSI/NISO Z39.48–1992 (R 1997) (*Permanence of Paper*).

FIRST AMERICAN EDITION

LIBRARY OF CONGRESS CATALOGING-IN-PUBLICATION DATA

Names: Wilkinson, J. Harvie, III, 1944– author.
Title: All falling faiths : reflections on the promise and failure of the 1960s / by J. Harvie Wilkinson III.
Description: New York : Encounter Books, 2017. | Includes bibliographical references and index.
Identifiers: LCCN 2016011695 (print) | LCCN 2016012167 (ebook) | ISBN 9781594038914 (hardcover : alk. paper) | ISBN 9781594038921 (Ebook)
Subjects: LCSH: Wilkinson, J. Harvie, III, 1944– | Judges—United States—Biography. | United States—Social conditions—1960–1980. | Law—Political aspects—United States—History—20th century. | Nineteen sixties.
Classification: LCC KF373.W4654 A3 2017 (print) | LCC KF373.W4654 (ebook) | DDC 347.73/2434—dc23
LC record available at http://lccn.loc.gov/2016011695

PRODUCED BY WILSTED & TAYLOR PUBLISHING SERVICES

To
My Beautiful Wife
and
My Beloved Country

Contents

Preface

They call us baby boomers. We have been misnamed. We are the Sixties Generation, who now with unaccustomed humility must beseech future generations to build back the nation we did much to tear down.

They have every right to tell us no. The world is very much a mess. Instantaneous information, immediate connectivity, often good and necessary in themselves, cloud our ability to make sense of it all. Ferguson, Baltimore; ISIS, 9/11; Dallas and Orlando; Ebola fears and rising seas cascade upon us. Our present worries foretell danger from which every human instinct is to hide; we await many an unpleasant surprise. There may be a rush to private havens, a willingness to abandon America to inevitability, a tendency to see hope and opportunity as bygone relics of a naïve age.

Two thousand sixteen became the new century's Year of Anger. Anger at whoever is different. Anger at whatever has changed. "Anger," write the *Washington Post*'s David Maraniss and Robert Samuels, "at Wall Street. Anger at Muslims. Anger at trade deals. Anger at Washington. Anger at police shootings of young black men. Anger at President Obama.

Anger at Republican obstructionists. . . . Specific anger and undefined anger and even anger about anger."

It has been building for a long time. *New York Times* columnist Frank Bruni notes that "for a solid decade the percentage of Americans who said that the United States was on the wrong track had exceeded the percentage who said it was on the right track," often by astounding and increasing numbers. He "wondered about a change in the very psychology and identity of a country once famous for its sunniness about tomorrows."

The mindset of eternal negativity is something the 1960s helped to load upon us. It is not a burden we should ever accept. The values the Sixties scorned; the chaos they engendered; the divisions they spawned—these are not our fates! Great enduring constants exist in this world that may yet guide us. From that burnt and ravaged forest of a decade may still spring the shoots of America anew.

But to overcome the Sixties, we must first understand them. One must sometimes first go back in time in order to move forward.

As a federal judge for more than thirty years and counting, I feel some days I've earned the right to reminisce. Maybe all my generation has.

But reminiscence is a mellow flight over a time, even a lifetime, amiably spent. No one should ever "reminisce" about the 1960s. Those years are memory's scorched earth.

I too am almost afraid to go back. That decade spared me none of itself: its lack of humor, its self-absorption, its fear of age, its resentment of authority, its rush to confrontation, its grim, bleating fret with the Establishment.

So why not leave those years behind? Because it was there—in the Sixties—that feelings toward home, work, school, church, and flag forever changed. The 1960s did not

end in 1970. They haunt us even now. Many Americans
sense the world unraveling around them and wonder why.
They want to know why they feel anxious about all that
awaits their children and grandchildren. There are many reasons why, but one of the big reasons is the 1960s.

It is too easy to blame all that happened in the 1960s
on student radicals. Certainly the mindless nihilism of the
radicals was destructive, but the radicals alone could not have
maimed our country. Those who were supposed to lead and
guide our nation—the generation that so inspired America in
the Depression and World War II—also abdicated their duty
and let us down in the 1960s.

Together, those who challenged authority and those
who exercised authority made the Sixties an experience in
lethal blindness. No one could see. The angry left saw no
good in America. The Establishment saw almost nothing bad.
No one foresaw the lasting damage the Sixties would inflict.
No one sensed the Sixties would shake our foundations even
today.

I know many Americans believe the 1960s was one of the
greatest decades ever. They believe that the decade made our
country more equal and more just: that African Americans
and eventually all minorities benefited more from the 1960s
than from any time since the Civil War; that women became
freer to make choices about home, children, husband, and
career than ever before; that Americans learned from the de-
bacle of Vietnam that the greatest power in the world could
overreach. Many good people think the 1960s accomplished
many good things, and I wholeheartedly agree with them.

Few decades did so much good for America as the 1960s.
But no decade inflicted so much continuing harm. The Sixties gave us some wonderful things, but this very gift has
caused us to downplay the decade's darker side. Righting

terrible social wrongs should never have come at such a horrible cost: so much lasting loss of faith in this great land.

In the 1960s, we lost much of the true meaning of education, much of our capacity for lasting personal commitments,
much of our appreciation for the rule of law, and much of
our sense of rootedness and home. We started to lose also the
sense of those things that are larger than ourselves: the desire
for service, the feeling for country, the need for God.

Many of those arguing about the 1960s today never lived
through them. To live in the Sixties was exhilarating at best,
but disturbing and harrowing most of the time. You enjoy
a ride on the roller coaster at the fair because you know the
ride will end. With the Sixties, we never knew. And the ride
goes on.

Yet it is important not to oversimplify. The term "Sixties" does not mean some dark sinister force of a decade
predestined to swamp all that followed it. Like any other
swath of history, the 1960s featured periods of normalcy between shattering events. Some days were mercifully ordinary.
It wasn't as though we never had time to sip milk shakes
through a straw. The decade wasn't all about sit-ins, marches,
riots, assassinations, war, and the other upheavals by which
we now mostly remember it. But the big happenings set the
tone and worked to inculcate attitudes that to a remarkable
degree govern how we see ourselves and our country today.
When I use the shorthand "Sixties," it is to describe that phenomenon and my amazement that any ten years would mark
such a turning point, that even at this very hour we see the
decade's imprint in so much of what we say and do.

Where are the shock troops of the Sixties now? Some
have no doubt mellowed and are planning cruises, collecting
dividends and pension checks, and carving Thanksgiving tur-
keys in the golden years that modern medicine and a senior-

solicitous political system have made possible. It's hard, after all, to stay radicalized into your seventies. If many of the long-ago activists have settled down, the society they created decidedly has not. Today's disunion bears the earmarks of our youth.

Much of the turmoil during the 1960s can be traced to the Cruel Swap. One instant John F. Kennedy was the pulse of hope; in the next, Lyndon Baines Johnson was the unwanted stepfather arriving on the doorstep to prosecute an unwanted war. Johnson, for all his domestic achievements, extinguished our belief in a world of possibility, and the backlash was profound. It is wisest, of course, not to get swept up by the transformative promises of charismatic presidents. But leadership matters, especially to the young, and the Cruel Swap set the tone of the decade's darkest years, leaving an entire spectrum of a generation feeling abysmally cheated and shortchanged.

I have gambled in making this a personal tale. So I should start with a personal confession. Perhaps the very last person who should be writing personally about the Sixties is a white, Protestant, Southern, and distinctly privileged male. I acknowledge the limitations of my own perspective and experience but hold out the hope that others may recognize the shortcomings of any singular perspective too. The losses inflicted by the Sixties have left no one out. They continue to touch every race, creed, gender, and class. In the end, I believe, the sense of loss and the urgency to overcome it will be something we come as Americans to share.

The issues posed by the 1960s will last long into our future. The vast damage of the decade must not leave us as a nation without hope. The three most inspiring figures of the 1960s—Martin Luther King, Jr., and John and Robert Kennedy—each had surpassing hope for this country. They remain figures whom we, in memoriam, dare not disappoint.

It is thus altogether good to embrace the Sixties' great achievement: that America belongs to all its citizens, not just some. It is altogether right to believe that the best days for our beautiful country lie ahead. But in order to do so, we must acknowledge the wreckage the Sixties left behind. Value by value, chapter by chapter, I hope to illuminate the depth of our loss, believing that a personal journal best reveals it. To recover our faith, we must revisit this loss. We must go back again.

All Falling Faiths

I. The Decline of Education

Bright College years, with pleasure rife,
The shortest, gladdest years of life. . . .

LONG AFTER we have forgotten all else about college, we remember the songs. The music strips away clutter. Call it nostalgia if you will, but the music touches a chord.

Sing the Whiffenpoofs assembled,
With their glasses raised on high,
And the magic of their singing casts its spell . . .

It is not a political message that music makes us remember. No, it is something infinitely less momentous than that. Some fleeting musical moment of friendship that we now wish could become precious and permanent.

Yale was rich in musical memory. Its singing groups were beyond number, and it was said to be a campus that could break forth in song. Song was part of the place that beckoned entering freshmen. I arrived in the fall of 1963, toting my college wish list. I wanted a varsity sweater, a Phi Beta Kappa key, a tap from Skull and Bones, a solo on the Whiffenpoofs—I wanted these things because they were the Yale I'd always dreamed about.

1

Of course, I mainly wanted to get an education. I'm not sure I knew exactly what my education should consist of, but Yale would take care of that. It would encourage questions and welcome inquiry. It would provide me with a mentor whose knowledge and wisdom would lead me through life. I expected all this, never dreaming that this great university would in many ways set the example of what education should not be.

Of all the damage done by the 1960s, that to education may be the worst. The early idealism of the Sixties often first appeared in colleges and universities, and the later disillusionment became the most intense in the halls of academia. The Sixties politicized everything they touched, most especially education. Eventually, no teacher, no class, no thought had any standing independent of politics. Every idea was filtered through the latest political crusade. The politicization of the campus became in time the politicization of the culture. The old adage—politics stops at the water's edge—became a bygone memory of bipartisanship. After the 1960s, politics stopped nowhere.

I entered the gates of college with few political thoughts in mind. College traditions back in 1963 gave us no warning of all that lay ahead. Yale echoed with the names of old New England places, Branford, Saybrook; of old New England men, Trumbull, Davenport, Edwards; of philanthropists of great vision or vanity, Harkness, Sterling, Peabody. There were the towers, cathedral Gothic; the columns, Georgian Colonial. On tables at Mory's were the etchings of long-dead students, on the walls the oars of some forgotten crew. And always the photographs of earlier Yale Men—in their stovepipe hats, vests, watch chains, bow ties, starched collars, and Chester Alan Arthur chops. Yale, on which the present trespassed: "Just who are you and your generation?"

But as we sang the old songs and walked the ancient corridors and courtyards, the old Yale was receding. It was not
just that the Computer Center now eclipsed some Gothic
archway or that the disheveled tenants of contemporary Yale
disdained their gallant ancestors. Yale had long since ceased to
be the finishing school for sons of the old WASP aristocracy.
The Old Blue might still drop his namesake at Andover, but
not so easily at Yale. In the class of 1940, the percentage of
alumni sons was 29; by 1971, it was 14. My own class (1967)
was the first with a majority of public high school graduates.

Life at college from the first was fervidly nocturnal. In
the early morning, we were useless; we staggered forth into
light to that gruesome first class. By afternoon, the sluggish-
ness disappeared; then night, when lights from rooms dot-
ted the campus into the wee hours, and the vault of restless
intellect was again alive. Now emotions broke their daytime
casts. Ideas sprang forth and friends were made. One hour's
conversation destroyed the country; the next more perfectly
reassembled it. By 2 A.M. life and mind were liquid; I watched
darting eyes and a haggard face extolling Rousseau to me in
some crummy all-nighter in New Haven.

There was in fact no more exciting place on earth than
Yale in the early 1960s. This excitement was essential to the
whole enterprise of education, and Yale had it in such abun-
dance that I miss it even now. What I only later understood
was that all this incessant, restless energy made college vul-
nerable to any idea that could claim to be New. New meant
Our Generation. To find good in the past was to brand oneself reactionary. The Sixties replaced critical thought with
a litmus test of novelty. New and old supplanted good and
bad, and new ideas invariably sought to level old values and
institutions.

This clamor for change shook every precinct of tradition.

None wore the cloak of change more strikingly than the Reverend William Sloane Coffin, Jr. Alumni loathed him, their vehemence his sustenance. Parents feared him, this cleric who would claim the souls of their sons. His words grabbed us, shook our conscience, demanded we forsake smug surroundings and posh backgrounds for the sharecroppers and ghetto-orphans of this world. Coffin was a bear of a man, with a face strong and vital, and an urgent, pungent voice. He plowed up pragmatists and gradualists with humanitarian zeal. He was for peace and against poverty—a born crusader in search of some new Satan to slay. "Yours must not be the world of black *against* white," he thundered, "but of black *and* white against injustice."

Because we so admired John F. Kennedy, we in the Sixties thought charisma a wonderful thing. Kennedy and the Sixties predisposed us utterly to personal magnetism, so long as it meant change. Coffin had causes to go with his charisma—some good, others terrible, all announced to fanfare, few submitted to reflection. If education means anything, it means being able to spot a demagogue. But Coffin's shock rhetoric absolutely swept us in.

Here was a clergyman and an academic, two callings that were supposedly "non-involved." The one attended to the affairs of God, the other to educating the young. Coffin spurned both views. "The Church should be like a moveable crap game," he announced. "Every morning it should wake up and ask where the action is today." Yale's chaplain followed the action. In 1961 he was a Freedom Rider challenging Alabama's segregated buses and terminals. In 1964 he led the citizens of India in prayer for Barry Goldwater's defeat. Indignant over Vietnam, he urged medical aid for the Vietcong and, later, that young men defy the draft to protest the war. Strident, combative, courageous, creative, he had the dominating energy of ebullient certitude.

Beside Coffin at the forefront of campus activism stood Staughton Lynd, then an assistant professor of history. In contrast to Coffin, Lynd was gentle, downright meek, but he had an ability even greater than Coffin's to communicate sincerity. It amazed me to hear this quiet, almost inaudible man contemplate such clamorous strategies. Lynd styled himself a Marxist-Pacifist-Quaker-Existentialist, which left him little in common with American law. But his primary allegiance, his upward eye reminded, was not to the law of the United States but to the higher law of his own conscience. "There is a place in the democratic process for people taking a position outside the law," he insisted. "This is how the law grows." Vietnam was his target. "If I were called upon to serve in what I considered an unjust war, I would refuse to serve— even if it meant going to jail."

If Coffin was a catalyst, Lynd was at first a curiosity. Not the kind of curiosity, mind you, at which to gaze and walk away. In fact, the more one pondered this calm curiosity, the more turbulent one became. As for authority, Lynd counseled "Disobey." As for the flag, Lynd accused America of crimes against humanity. He was an affront to twenty years of assumptions, a dare to rethink it all again.

He opposed American involvement in Vietnam from the outset, when student deferments wrapped Yale in a cocoon. In 1965, he withheld taxes to protest "an immoral war." Next, he visited Hanoi in defiance of a State Department ban. On his return, with the government revoking his passport and the Old Blues demanding his hide, Lynd stepped before a packed throng at Woolsey Hall. "Whether or not Yale keeps me or fires me," he said, "is insignificant compared to what we will be doing to the Vietnamese ten days from now." Woolsey Hall erupted; Yale awoke. I sat there, stunned by his humble arrogance, drawn to his lonely audacity, one man whispering that millions were insane.

Nothing was beyond question then. No belief was certain. When they first burst on the scene, Lynd and Coffin seemed to represent what was good in education—fresh thought, moral courage, an insistence on matching American rhetoric with reality, be it in Birmingham or Saigon. The irony was that those who rightly challenged the assumptions of others became slowly more indignant at any challenge to their own. But schools of thought that turn intolerant rarely start that way. The idealists first summon the sons of man to their utopia only if the sins of the fathers can be slain.

The decade in its early years was like that—one of unsurpassed exhilaration. The surge of idealism, the sense of possibility, were everywhere. Life was gathered into the simple words of brotherhood and peace. Yale's blueprint for society was itself a sparkling blue. If America didn't have a solution, it was only because Yale had yet to shed its light upon the problem. The call for change came as never before. We Yalies were missionaries, possessed, as we were, of learned heads and earnest hearts. If we had done something different to get to Yale, we had to make a difference while at Yale. The torch had indeed passed to a new generation—our own. In the face of such a calling, the traditional pursuits of college life came to seem quite antique.

Not to my father, though. Yale was *my* choice; it was never his. Princeton was pastoral and Wilsonian and still south of New York, the northernmost promontory where a Virginian could go and still maintain respectability. "And I must pay to lease you to the devil?" Father groaned, upon hearing "Yale." His brow furrowed with incomprehension.

He saw in Yale a bit of a reproach, as though the way he had raised me was no longer good enough, that I had to seek something different and alien.

Father insisted that I pledge a fraternity. I'd be a Brother first and foremost, he swore. "My friends were all DKEs or Phi Kaps at heart." But fraternities were full of high-school juvenility, like rush and hazing—six were all that remained at Yale.

To humor him, I joined St. Anthony Hall. Like a little gray castle it stood, at the corner of College and Wall. It had a bar, weekend parties, and continental breakfast every morning. To call St. Anthony's a flesh-and-booze frat wouldn't be quite fair. It was more like a society than a fraternity, in fact. Every Thursday night, the Brothers gathered in fellowship and under oath of secrecy to talk.

St. Anthony Hall was out of step with the Sixties. It was a relic where friendship grew as slowly as the ivy on its stone gray walls. Because I joined the place only to indulge a parent, I skipped the parties and discussions alike. There was no point to St. Anthony Hall, except the indecent exposure of leisure to a hurried world. There was no point to a fraternity party: Yale had passed the last such remnants of idle pleasures by.

I never learned until too late that to require a point can sometimes be to miss the point. That St. Anthony Hall had no point beyond friendship was its strength. College is the only time we have to savor thoughts and people pointlessly— that is, for themselves.

Of course, there was always the Musical Yale. Shortly after arriving, I saw a tryout notice for the freshman glee club. There was a freshman everything then, a buffer from the gale force of Yale. Freshmen even lived together on the Old Campus, an ivied fortress, starkly self-contained. I was to report to a separate freshman dean, sleep in a freshman dorm, eat freshman food at commons, play freshman sports, and—if I could make it—sing freshman songs in the freshman glee club.

"Read music?" asked the director, at my tryout.

"Not so well."

"No problem," he said, sitting at the piano. "Everyone knows this," and he began to play "Aura Lee."

"A first tenor," he exclaimed. "Fantastic! First tenors are choice. We'll have fun. Hold joint concerts. You'll learn music and meet some fetching soprano in the deal."

I never did. I went to several practices, but I never really entered in. I was taking a course in ideology—John Stuart Mill to Karl Marx. I was studying philosophy—Plato and Kant. I was debating the Cold War and missile build-ups. Songs came to seem like lace Valentines, sentiments that serious minds disdained. So I gave him the excuse we often give—no time.

"You're not disappointed?" I said, as he sat there, silent.

"No," he said quietly. "It's your life without music, not mine."

No time! No time! That became the Sixties' mantra. The ills of society had to be purged yesterday. Beauty only dulled the sense of purpose, so I never took a course in music or in art. I can't go to a museum now without wondering about those courses I missed back in college. But then I had resisted. "Appreciation" was the language of leisure. Besides, Bach and Vermeer never changed the course of history; education in the Sixties above all meant no frills.

Saturday afternoons still tried to buck the grim tide of social relevance. They were doggedly reserved for football. The team slumped during my four years there; we would beat Brown and Columbia early in the season only to lose to Dartmouth, Princeton, and Harvard. Ivy League football was more spirited than most because it was less professional. I would cover my eyes as the team devised some new species of blunder. I wanted most to defeat Princeton: its band fluttered about in prim little jackets of black and orange "tiger" stripes. But invariably we lost, and I tried to sneak out of the stadium ahead of those on the other side.

Mostly, however, football didn't matter. It was there on Saturday afternoons, and then it was gone. It would have been healthy for the team to have had some Monday morning quarterbacks—those who second-guess at least continue to care. The Football Weekend—the crowds, the mascots, the bands, the cheerleaders—all that seemed a waste of time too. The game became chiefly the preoccupation of those who played it, and of alumni who recalled the Glory Days. This was a shame, because the players played their hearts out:

> Middle of the second quarter, Yale's ball on its own 15. First and ten. Ball snapped. Hand off to Mercein! Moves off tackle. Side-steps one tackler, shakes another, two linebackers converge, slow him, he's hit, but he struggles, great second effort and dives forward for a 5-yard gain.

It was reported afterward that Chuck Mercein's leg swelled so much that his pants had to be cut off him with scissors. The fact was not much noticed. Yale by the mid-Sixties had passed into the post-heroic age.

Fall passed into winter. Yale became a gray, heavy fortress under a low, sullen sky. New Haven recalled the old hymn: "Frosty wind made moan." Soon the streets and sidewalks were puddled and slushed, and we moved slowly, funereally along them. Always a bandaged man on a corner: "A dime for some coffee, sir?" But we were seldom outside; rather the slap-slap of sneakers on the gym floor. In the early dark, we retired to the static of the dining halls. Midwinter exams: I had a cold and studied in my room with the stale air, unmade bed, and scattered papers, and the chair losing its stuffing. Studying was such slow stuff—being a mere student in the Sixties was allowing the world to pass you by.

If anything could have, February at Yale would have turned me to drugs or alcohol. Most of my friends drank freely enough; a number smoked pot; a few took LSD. And why not? If the Sixties were to be an experiment in bold new ideas, why not in bold new drugs? If the decade was to alter the consciousness of mankind, why not make an alteration in personal consciousness as well? A fraternity brother swore I could never hope to know true color without taking LSD. More than an aesthetic adventure, LSD was supposed to offer insight that the slow laborious educational process couldn't touch. If drugs as education sounded vague, well, you had to hallucinate to find out. "Turn on, tune in, drop out," was educator Timothy Leary's motto. Since the Sixties meant to see all things and people differently, LSD became the drug of the decade—the perfect, exquisite match.

I was hopelessly behind in the hallucinogenic category, because I hadn't even learned to drink. Father, in the tradition of the family, had offered me a gold watch and $1,000 if I would not drink or smoke until my twenty-first birthday. I was eighteen before I thought much about it. Then, when I did, I realized I was almost there.

My abstinence incensed my friends. How could I do this to them? Not only was I wronging them by not drinking—in the end I was cheating only myself. In short, they thought I had sinned and should quickly mend my ways.

My twenty-first birthday came—too quickly. Upon arriving at Mory's, I saw that what I intended as an intimate affair had ripened into a mob. Bucky, who appointed himself master of ceremonies, set the ground rules for the evening. I, of course, could drink as much or as little as I pleased, but as a point of courtesy, everyone personally toasted was expected to imbibe greatly in appreciation.

The first four toasts were to me. My friends were now whipping around a mixture of which crème de menthe was the major ingredient. Someone thumped my back to congratulate me on my "buzz." "Here, take this," Chip called. "Coke's soothing on an upset stomach." But the Coke, to everyone's knowledge and delight, turned out to be Coke and rum, and my insides sped down the road to disaster. Two (or was it three?) friends carted me home, where I rested my eyes, my head hanging over the latrine. Then to bed, where my stomach whimpered and my room spun wildly around me. I hardly remember turning twenty-one.

That birthday was about the best time I had. How strange that I should think that. I was as sick as could be. How could I come to take pleasure in what were truly miserable moments? At college, lightheartedness was at best a diversion—at worst an affront. At my birthday, I had no time to think about it.

It wasn't that Yale eliminated sports and fraternities, only frowned upon them. Perhaps it should have. Perhaps good times at college have nothing to do with anything—maybe such laughter should be gone with the wind. Yet if life is a gift as well as a test, not all joy is selfish, not all pleasure is to be condemned.

What I never fully realized at college is that one can learn through laughter—about oneself and others and all sorts of things. Smiles open us up to one another in a way that stern features never do. In the Sixties we rightly began to realize the value of diversity—the need to know people quite different from ourselves. But how odd that the decade that introduced us to diversity made us too damn uptight to experience it. In the Sixties we forgot that education that is only in dead earnest kills personal exploration too. Learning through laughter was too often lost to us then—even now diversity seems to be pursued in mere theory without the joy that could bring it to life.

But that was college then—more serious and purposeful by the hour. Late in my freshman year I joined the Yale Political Union. It began to seem unthinkable not to spend my college years in public debate. The Political Union was then Yale's largest extracurricular organization, with more than five hundred members, whose views ranged from Birchite to Communist. Its alumni boasted William Scranton, Robert Taft, Jr., McGeorge and William Bundy, John Lindsay, and Potter Stewart; most of the Old Blues were moderate, Republican, and respectable. The Political Union had no honorarium to offer speakers, but many wanted to come to Yale: *New York Times* columnist James Reston, natty, low-key, was the most interested in what we were thinking; South Carolina Senator Strom Thurmond wanted to race us to the meeting hall; Draft Director Lewis Hershey, avuncular, gesticulative, tried to say, "Now, no one's going to mug you boys"; Assistant Secretary of State William Bundy was a patrician pleader for Lyndon Baines Johnson; Michael Harrington, a fount of ideas for the frontier left; James Farmer, of CORE, massive, arrogant, supremely eloquent; Roy Wilkins, of the NAACP, urbane, humble, sincere, and out of fashion with black students.

I became increasingly involved in the organization's politics. It was a byzantine world of thirty-odd positions to be filled anew each semester. Often there were more candidates than constituents, so eagerly did student politicos play musical chairs for petty office. Some in this wild world learned the value of loyalty, the delicacies of patronage (whose names should go on the official stationery?), the hazards (and merits) of indecision, the aim of paying attention to everyone all the time. Student politics could also be bitter. The opposing factions of the Yale Republican Club were not on speaking terms, and swore to annihilate each other should their political paths ever cross in later life.

At the Political Union, I got to know John Kerry. We lived a stone's throw from each other in Jonathan Edwards, one of Yale's residential colleges. John was class of '66; I was class of '67. We both wanted to be president of the Union and together we hit upon a coalition ticket as the way to do it. John would run for president, and I for vice president. John would get his Liberal Party behind the ticket, and I would get Conservative Party backing for it. The next year, I'd run for president with the same set of forces. We each kept our end of the deal, and things worked out as planned.

When I say I "got to know" John through the Political Union, that was an exaggeration. We were both too driven to get to know the person behind the political transaction. Friendship seemed so incidental to what we were about. John's room was festooned with pictures of sailing outings with the Kennedys; it was no secret his initials were JFK. If John stood aloof with his endless Kennedy affectations, he was trustworthy and true to his word. When he ran for president in 2004 against George Bush, class of '68, it was hard to believe the two men had ever been in the same place at the same time. Each had sidestepped the Sixties in a different way, Kerry because he was entirely focused on his own advancement, Bush because he was not focused on anything much at all. I recollect him as a nice guy with whom I'd occasionally enjoy pitching football. Bush was so easygoing; he mocked the whole decade.

I never really kept up with Kerry or Bush after Yale. My

few contacts with each were brief and cursory until President
Bush invited me to the White House in 2005 for an interview for a vacancy on the Supreme Court.

The president was the same decent man I remembered
from college, and he put me at ease. Not so much at ease,
however, that I wished to discuss Yale or the Sixties or anything of the sort. It would have been interesting to know
what Bush thought about the decade, how Yale had affected
him, whether there were positive lessons to be drawn from
those years, but I was not about to touch it. Bush's daughter
Barbara was a Yale undergraduate, and the president would
sometimes invite classmates to an occasion at the White
House. But caring for his classmates as individuals was one
thing, and an affinity with Yale as an institution or the Sixties as a decade was something else. I sensed the president
had left it long ago. So Yale had to be acknowledged, but
nothing more than that. I mentioned to the president how
much I'd liked his roommate, Bob McCallum, and that I'd
played briefly on the tennis team. Bush spoke warmly of Bob,
who served in his administration, and with that we left Yale
behind. Interviews, after all, should not seek out painful
subjects.

The tennis team, which I had felt safe in mentioning,
had been fun. In my sophomore year, over spring break, the
team toured Florida. I was the caboose, the tenth man on
a ten-man roster. At the University of Miami, the students
ate outside all winter; the bulletin boards announced aquatic
pleasures, not political protests. I had forgotten how it felt
to be outdoors all day and, after five sets of singles, to soak
with wonderful soreness in a whirlpool. At night, pale Yalies
sought Miami coeds, the better to take the balmy air. Next
day, tennis again. The Yalies got clobbered, of course; we

were unaccustomed, so we said, to playing cheek to jowl with the equator. But I was happy, devoting myself to swatting a ball. Each day I played until my arm swung out on me. All I asked of life was a crisp, crosscourt backhand.

So life beyond politics did occur in the Sixties, but any glimpse I had would prove very brief indeed. Back at Yale, another Political Union campaign awaited me, this one for president. For a month and a half before the election, my opponent and I worked four to five hours a day—cutting deals, meeting voters, speaking out—doing everything to gain support. The race drew close; every ounce of effort mattered. I began to miss tennis practice. The coach called: had I been ill? There was no time, I explained, to study, to politic, and to play tennis. Forced to choose, I quit the tennis team.

What in heaven's name made me give up these things— the glee club, the tennis team, the fine arts classes, and, yes, even the fraternity parties? One after another, I passed up what I now wish I could go back and do. I am not longing for lost youth; rather, I regret the youth I never had. It isn't bygone times I grieve, but times that never were.

This was especially the case with education. We began to lose faith even in our courses. Some professors at Yale were remote. Some were too shy; some were too busy; some sensed that respect required distance. Some—such as C. Vann Woodward, Frederick Watkins, and Cleanth Brooks—seemed persons of great substance and quiet charm. For them, ideas were not engines raced to each day's new debate; polemic gave way to a longer, steadier ride. Woodward in particular was a grand master of words. His was the story of the Southern people, and he moved behind that land's romantic haze to tell of poverty, defeat, and prejudice, and the region's slow and faltering struggle to shed them. Watkins spoke of the rise and fall of ideologies, of how brilliant and magnetic men sought to move peoples behind bold systems of ideas, only to watch their systems crack and fissure because people were as they were, not as ideology told them they should be. Brooks showed us a poem—not a meandering stream of lovely lines, but a total and unitary impression to which meter, metaphor, and individual words contributed— in short, the "well wrought urn."

These teachers should have been icons, so much wisdom was gathered up within them. But the Sixties had little time for village elders—elders required listening and the Sixties meant to shout. Education became a process of unmistakable messaging and of one directional bent. In Professor John Morton Blum's classroom, the robber baron poses for a portrait with his greatcoat; the poor shiver in their tenements. Railroads, steel plants, automobiles, and oil wells dynamize America. But tycoons are men of scurvy habit; their smokestacks foul the air; their greed chokes small competitors; their factories and mills wear down young girls before their time. Toady presidents do the bidding of business. Callous philosophers rationalize its course. Despoiled land, fictitious stock, and contaminated nutriment attend its progress. The Great Depression followed from its sin.

I left Blum confused. Was all wealth suspect? Did success require a censored conscience? Over whose numbed backs had Yale's own benefactors climbed? How had my forebears secured my blessings? What must I, their offspring, now do to make amends?

How, I used to wonder, would Blum explain the businessmen I knew back home? They were decent to their families. They donated to charity. They went each Sunday to their pew at church. Father had never been too busy to give the community his time. How did these people do the things Blum said? Were friends of Father warm to me and cold to others not my class? Would Yale unleash us, snarling, on our backgrounds? Or just throw everything—and everyone—into everlasting question?

It seems unfair in one sense to single out Blum. He was a gifted teacher whose voice boomed across the lecture hall, almost dwarfing the spiffy little man in bow tie behind the lectern. But Blum's fondness for such phrases as "ruthless industrial corporations" and "hoary tenets of free enterprise" imparted a faint air of disrepute to the entire private sector. With President Kennedy extolling the ideal of public service and with college professors belittling American business, is it any wonder that so many of us thought more of the Peace Corps than of GM?

This disdain of the Sixties for the private sector is one of many things that has assisted the unimpeded growth of government to this day. We had rather be caught dead than be a vice president of a bank, or a utility, or, God forbid, a life insurance company. Such jobs, which had served our parents and communities well, were for the dull and plodding souls of prior generations. I myself became a law professor, a journalist, a Justice Department lawyer, and a federal judge. Perhaps those choices were all from natural inclination, but the Sixties scared me away from any thought of a career in business. When you say what you are doing, you want your peers to be impressed, and many of my classmates thought of CEOs as dreary sell-outs.

Education, of course, is all about trying different things. To the extent that Yale made me question my background, I owe it a lot. To the extent that Yale made us all rethink American history, such a reassessment was overdue. But there is a difference between being taught to question and being trained to hate. The hatred of the Sixties spread from the present to the past. Because the Sixties confronted so much racism in the struggle for civil rights and so much imperialism in the war in Vietnam, it followed from the ugly events of the present that the American past required an apology too.

Before the Sixties, the essential good of American history outshone its admitted faults. After the Sixties, oppression overshadowed everything—history was how America mistreated working classes and the minorities in its midst. But alongside the shameful chapters of slavery and segregation and the sordid betrayals of Native Americans lies a glorious tale of an experiment with constitutional liberty that has endured and worked. In its reluctance to tell the good side of the American story, the Sixties made its own contribution to the historical illiteracy that afflicts us today. No one wants hagiography, to be sure, but if our own history is to become one extended exercise in self-flagellation, what child, or adult for that matter, will ever take much joy in the study of it?

This point was brought home to me when my old friend Henry Abraham, a political science professor at the University of Virginia, delivered a speech in 2014 on Holocaust Remembrance Day. It was not an easy speech for him to give, but this is what he had to say: His mother, a lady of "steel wrapped in silk," had "fought my father tooth and nail to let me leave Nazi Germany alone for the States" in 1937 at age fifteen, "thus giving me life twice—once at my birth and once to send me off to America." His parents and younger brother managed to join him in Pittsburgh in 1939, barely "avoiding the fate of extermination of sixteen close family members in the concentration camps, gas chambers, and ovens in multiple horror locations, such as Auschwitz. For me a new life loomed in America, for which I have been eternally grateful: school, work, college (including an Episcopal one), teaching, marriage, children and grandchildren, university, travelling, writing," and so much else. As World War II came, Henry "served in United States Army intelligence and the armed forces that retook Germany, including the town of Offenbach am Main, where I was born." We "should all be eternally grateful to the Supreme Allied Commander, General Dwight D. Eisenhower, who not only insisted that all military personnel abroad become physically familiar" with the Nazi concentration camps, "but that all America would learn of the Holocaust we remember today." To forget is to exonerate, and that is why tales of personal abuse and subjugation under slavery must be remembered. It's just that journeys like my friend's went unmentioned in the rants of the Sixties, and Henry's story is part of the American story too.

The war on American history begun in the Sixties continues today with the War on Names—the rising impulse to redesignate colleges, schools, stadiums, dormitories, professorships, or lecture series that bear the name of some prominent figure who carries the stigma of some long-discredited practice in some long-ago time. It is entirely reasonable to argue that Yale's Calhoun College should not bear the name of a particularly raw and virulent exponent of the "rights" of slaveholders and secessionists. But where does it end? Tradition has a coinage of its own. Many past figures, like ourselves, had their admirable and regrettable moments in life, and other generations, like our own, will be frowned upon by those who follow. Justice Oliver Wendell Holmes, one of the greatest figures in all of American law, lies trapped forever in the irony of abjuring Herbert Spencer's callous theory of "survival of the fittest" and declaring, in a bow to the notorious abuses of eugenics, that "three generations of imbeciles are enough." Should the much-respected Oliver Wendell Holmes Lectures at Harvard no longer bear his name?

As the Sixties wore on, education seemed to be coming apart. Knowledge for its own sake was devalued, because it bore no discernible relationship to political commitment or cause. The Sixties rejected education unconnected to the day and the hour. Who cared about my college courses? What did Othello know about the war in Vietnam? What, pray tell, had poems and novels to teach Yale? School seemed "irrelevant," to use the favorite word of the Sixties, and selfishly so. Not to feel relevant was to feel helpless, at a time when help was needed as never before.

What grated also was the sheer length of education. For my grandfather, high school had been okay; for Father, a college degree was enough. For me, graduate school was a necessity. The road ahead stretched endlessly, and I despaired of walking it. I was restless, not feeling anything tangible, not doing anything practical, not making any bit of difference. I remember so often just wanting my education to be over. The sooner I got my hands on the world, the better. Yet here I was biding my time, over-preparing for adulthood, slouching on my sofa, suffering the sight of windowpanes.

We all felt this welling restlessness, as if the interminable schooling were not preparing us for anything, but only holding us back from our rightful hour in the sun. Each vented in his own way. Some went to the battlements and sought a course of insubordination, an irretrievable break, a slap at the fixed face of authority, much like privileged peasants confronting the Czar's crack troops with frigid gaze. All of us, however, were swept up in the tides of social consciousness

that commenced modestly enough, but as the Sixties progressed became an all-consuming rage.

One felt this relentless need for relevance in moments
large and small. I remember that on the night before my
exam in geology, I decided to read a book on everyone's lips:
The Other America, by Michael Harrington. It would have ap-
palled my family—not to mention my old schoolmasters—to
learn I read about injustice the evening before an examination on ancient rock formations. If I absolutely had to read
Harrington, why risk my future doing it? But that was the
only time to do it: at some small risk to oneself.

"The American city," wrote Harrington,

> has been transformed. The poor still inhabit the miserable
> housing in the central area, but they are increasingly isolated
> from contact with, or sight of, anybody else. Middle-class
> women coming in from Suburbia on a rare trip may catch
> the merest glimpse of the other America on the way to an
> evening at the theater, but their children are segregated in
> suburban schools. The business or professional man may
> drive along the fringes of slums in a car or bus, but it
> is not an important experience to him. The failures, the
> unskilled, the disabled, the aged, and the minorities are
> right there, across the tracks, where they have always
> been. But hardly anyone else is.

Might ours, we all wondered, be a New Age of human
oneness between black and white, rich and poor, university idealist and oppressed Vietnamese? Was the Mississippi
sharecropper happy? The Vietnamese peasant? The Ap-
palachian miner? The Roxbury tenant? Then, asked Yale,
what right had we to be? Happiness was a selfish state, a false
state, while suffering so pained one's fellow man. How do

the poor hear ballroom laughter? How does the flophouse
hobo see my home? What joke had God played on us, the
children of privilege? He gave us everything, and then, with
human suffering, made the enjoyment of anything immoral
and impossible.

The Sixties waged incessant war on our minds and on
our backgrounds. I came to college proud of where I'd come
from, only to be told to be ashamed. Back home, there were
wine glasses, liqueur cups, crystal water glasses, raised in tin-
kling toasts to indifference. When I left college, when I grew
too old or too busy to read Michael Harrington, would those
be my toasts too? I used to see myself at fifty, prosperous,
sipping vintage wines, drowsily chatting with fireside friends,
well respected all. A true Virginia gentleman, bred to velvet
leisure, twilight charms, and a gentleman's success of boards,
clubs, and charities. Of what consequence!

No! A student in the Sixties had to understand what mattered—and what mattered was an outlook on the world that
was becoming angrier by the day. The extent of the anger
left little room for disagreement—out of the depths of disillusionment a bitter orthodoxy formed. As the Sixties progressed, the breeze of change became the hot breath of intolerance. Yale itself became less a place for original thought
than an intellectual inferno policed for its allegiance to the
prevailing alienation.

Many at Yale preferred to suppress speech rather than
respond to it. Education left increasingly less room to disagree. The campus turned hostile, first to defenders of segregated schools and then to proponents of the Vietnam War.
Governor George Wallace of Alabama scheduled a tour of
the East to promote the so-called Southern point of view on
school segregation. One stop was to be Yale. The provost

and leading candidate for the presidency of Yale at the time was Kingman Brewster, Jr. A former professor of law at Harvard and a former chairman of the *Yale Daily News*, Brewster asked the Political Union to disinvite Wallace "in the interest of law and order as well as town-gown relations." After meeting with Brewster, the Political Union declared that the "likelihood of uncontrolled civil disaster" required that Wallace stay away.

How sad that this talented and decent man bought a moment of peace and adulation by imbuing the liberal arts with lasting illiberal dogmas. Much of the faculty bridled at what historian C. Vann Woodward termed the sacrifice of "principle to expediency." A Committee for the Protection of Not Very Nice People formed in Yale Law School. Wallace was invited back to speak, but he declined. For me, a Southerner, the issue hit home. I dreaded being linked to the likes of Wallace but fumed that my region had been singled out for selective censorship by Yale. If the First Amendment meant anything, it meant that ugliness would discredit itself upon display and that shabby characters like George Wallace had a right to be heard.

As president of the Political Union, I invited a United States Senator from the Deep South—Allen J. Ellender of Louisiana—to Yale. I resented the senator's racial outlook, but I was determined to see the Wallace episode redeemed. A week before his arrival, the *Yale Daily News* announced that a bigot was coming to talk, and Ellender stepped into a packed and angry scene. The senator had brought color slides from his trips to Africa, not so subtly designed to laud the continent's colonial governments and to show native Africans as unprepared for self-rule. It would have been easy enough to demolish the senator's views with questions and opposing argument, but the evening took a different tack. "There's no place here for snakes," Ellender snapped, when hissing disrupted his slide show. Later, he was jeered, booed, and shouted down by seething questioners. As he swept up his slides and made for the exit, students jostled him and shook fists in his face. The atmosphere hovered a remark or two from a serious riot. Afterward I wrote him and apologized for the shoving he received. Ellender hadn't minded: a rude reception in New Haven only helped him in Baton Rouge.

The Ellender affair bore sour fruit. "Why'd you bring him here?" a classmate accosted me.

"He has a right to be heard. Same as you."

"I don't believe that."

"What do you mean?"

"I mean you brought him here because you agreed with him. Genteel folk won't soil their hands with his message, but you wished it said all the same."

I protested in vain. It did no good to say that Southern whites should not be stereotyped when, beneath the boot of Southern law, Southern blacks were ground the same. Now we stood to reap the whirlwind of our own oppression—wholesale. At Yale, my drawl made me suspect, a lightning rod for hostile comment over coffee, someone for whom disclaimers failed. Was a Southerner someone who must retire to his room, there to scrape his soul of racial algae, to scrub his spirit clean? The Ellender event had seemed so straightforward to me: Free Speech at Yale. Southern senators deserved First Amendment rights just as Southern blacks deserved the long-denied protections of the Fourteenth. We Southerners at Yale were no backward generation—we held no slaves, we wore no sheets, we watched no lynching bees. Yet Yale marked us as members of a malefactor race, a privileged race, our pathways cleared by history's hissing blade. And our children? Bequeath advantage—bequeath the shame!

The assault on study continued apace. Yale had much to offer, more to teach than any place I'd ever seen. But education there was now to be outside the classroom. The real learning was to take place on the sidewalks and the streets. Just about anything was worth a demonstration. And some of these demonstrations were actually for the good. Students were now marching against the food at college dining halls and for coeducation. They marched for Richard J. Bernstein, a small, intense teacher of philosophy who modernized Plato by imagining his dialogues with Yale students at the Old Heidelberg Restaurant in New Haven. But Bernstein let his typewriter gather dust, and tenure was denied him. "BERNSTEIN DROPPED: PROTESTS BREAK OUT," headlined the *Yale Daily News*, and a student vigil began outside President Brewster's office. "WHY NOT CREATIVE TEACHING? . . . COULD SOCRATES GET TENURE?" shouted students who mourned the loss of a great teacher and who worried not what his philosopher peers believed. "We are producing a generation of scholars who prefer to provide definitive answers to small questions rather than tentative answers to important ones," James Billington lamented. And Bernstein asked the important questions. The vigil ran around the clock, with a low of ten participants, but it ended with nearly a thousand.

Yale in 1967 was calmer than the Yale of 1970, when nine Black Panthers, including chairman Bobby Seale, went on trial for murder in New Haven. That was the spring of Nixon's thrust into Cambodia, and of Jerry Rubin's visit to Yale, and Tom Hayden's, and David Dellinger's, and Abbie Hoffman's: "Old man Brewster thinks he put one over on us. Shit, he doesn't know his ass from his elbow. We could tear

this place down in ten minutes—if we wanted to." Rumors
flew of caches of arms and bombs, and of violence by anti-
black vigilantes. "Free Bobby Seale! Free Bobby Seale! Free
Bobby Seale!"—the Panthers had the place by the tail and in
an uproar.

By my senior year (1966–1967), Yale was warming toward this frenzy. Already "strike" and "pig" had stoked the
vocabulary. Already there was stone-cold hatred for the war
and the president. HANDS-OFF-FOREIGN-CIVIL-WARS read one
placard; another, TELEGRAPH THE PRESIDENT! DEMAND AN END
TO VIETNAM! Even now, just before sleep, Yale comes into
memory as a train of student protesters—perhaps a multitude,
more often just a motley few, perhaps joyful, more often
weary and quarrelsome, perhaps for the war, much more often against it—but always, the sign with red, vampire letters—V I E T N A M.

In the end, thanks to the war, Yale became a place of
childlike clarity. I arrived at a university that asked questions;
I left one that fastened a creed. Good and bad, right and
wrong, us and them, in neon on high. The police were bad;
the banks and corporations were bad; the United States government was bad; the rich were bad; ROTC was bad. "Abbie Hoffman will point to every tall building and say, 'Fuck
that and fuck that and fuck that'" . . . and Yale obliged. "I
am skeptical of the ability of black revolutionaries to achieve
a fair trial anywhere in the United States," said President
Brewster. The Bulldog and the Panther, at one in alienation,
brothers under siege.

So had Yale taught me nothing, if not to hate? To hate
my background, my region, my affluence, my whole oppressive country? Lift the veils; smash the statues; strip privilege
of its pomp; sense the worst of those in power: is that educa-

tion? Yale dismantled—whatever else it did, it had no peer in destruction. Yale's litany of malice: prejudice in our laws, poverty in our ghettos, death in distant rice paddies—was there nothing, no one, left to believe? Peace, justice, equality—all in the end became transmuted into hate, hatred for those who held back the millennium, hatred for those who made our country what it was.

Hatred sown, perhaps, our first fall in college. No sooner did we get there than John Kennedy was killed. Suddenly, a parched field and dry wind and gaunt branches bent low in prayer and mourning. Our tongues were stripped of words; our minds laid bare of thought; our eyes baked dry of tears. Grief blew, like the tumbleweed, across us; anger swept, like a sheet of fire, through us; fear crashed, like a molten wall, upon us . . . on our college years would always lie the untimely ash of death, and death's surmise: "What if John Kennedy had lived?"

My last fall at college I just wanted out. I wanted the education that had eluded me thus far. I also wanted freedom from grades, from exams, from required courses, indeed from courses and classes altogether. It was no longer enough to dress or drive or date as I pleased. I wanted time to meditate, time to know myself, time to think and feel. Most of all, I wanted distance from the blast heat of Yale.

I joined the Scholar of the House Program, which relieved eighteen seniors of all class and course work. At the end of the year I had to turn in a thesis, but until then my time was completely my own. Students worked all year in their fields of special interest: photography, jazz, dinosaur bones, movie making, Attic pottery among them. My project was more conventional: a twentieth-century history of Virginia. I hoped this project would return me to the state I

knew and loved. At the beginning, the director tipped me off
on freedom: "Dangerous. A worse inebriant than alcohol."
Those with creative talents, he thought, were most prone
to despondency; he anticipated at least one crisis every year.
Would-be novelists learned they were not James Joyce, but
handling one's mediocrity was maturing, he believed. Gently he would adjust our aspirations. "He's lost his fire," we
complained.

It felt weird, being free of all routine. I was light, without gravity, tumbling through time. I cut all ties to clocks. I
dined at midnight, fell asleep at four, and read what books,
took what naps, attended what debates, lectures, and concerts
I pleased. I fit company to mood. Before my friends, I strut-
ted my ease.

But time turned on me. At first my emancipator, it became my albatross, something perpetual to justify, something
continual one must use. I began to hate my backpack of freedom, my incoherent nights and days. I returned, despite myself, to schedules: ten hours at the desk a day. By spring, I was
falling further behind, missing chapter deadlines, working
evenings and weekends, watching my classmates lunching
on the grass. I resolved my crisis by refocusing my history.
The proposed twentieth-century history of Virginia traversed
scarcely twenty years.

"We are the new youth," a friend announced to me
shortly before graduation. And what with the new protests,
the new dress, the new rhetoric, the new commitment, the
new insight, the new daring, the new anger, for a moment
I supposed him right. But youth always thinks itself new.
One night I returned to some old voices—poets bemused by
youthful rashness. There they were, ornate, sentimental, with
their mythical symbolism and their sermonizing. Predictably

they warned my youthful self against "dissipation" and "riot-
ousness" and above all against the "formation of evil habits."
"He who spends his younger days in dissipation," cautioned
one stern, metaphoric soul, "is mortgaging himself to disease
and poverty, two inexorable creditors, who are certain to
foreclose at last, and take possession of the premises." And
then those endless songs to "the pleasant spring of life when
joy is stirring in the dancing blood."

I laughed at the wooden moralists. But they made me feel
different. Where had it gone—this spring of life—the Glee
Club and the tennis team, the friendships, the follies, the tin-
gling of years soaring so free that one could never hope to
cage them? There were no parents, no children, no creditors,
no clients, no one to make us feel old and responsible. Only
a war, which managed to age us most of all.

My college years seemed so different from those of Father's reminiscences, when he stretched back of an evening
and spoke of times when . . . Students in his day dressed
up, not down, for occasions. College was the things you
got away with and the times you got caught. No cause or
crusade molested the campuses back in 1927, at least none
worth remembering. There were professors (to whom Father tipped his hat); deans (before whom Father repented);
fraternity blasts, gymnasium dances, food fights at Miss Lelia
Smith's, and a motto: "Prohibition is better than no liquor
at all." Father always said the follies a man misses most in his
life are those he failed to commit when he had the opportunity. College was that opportunity, as long ago as the days of
scolding poets, obsolete we thought, all because in the era
of new youth, they assumed it was still springtime.

"But Yale made you aware," my friend Doug said.

"Yes."

"Showed you good times."

"A few."

"So?"

"So, there's no listening here any longer. There's only Yale-Think."

Doug looked perplexed. His dark hair fell in a mop down his ears and forehead. He reclined, raising his feet in untied tennis shoes.

"It ain't Yale's fault, Jay. After all, Yale's not shooting peasants. Yale ain't keeping blacks out of anybody's school. The ghetto ain't Yale's doing either. It's not Yale; it's what Yale wants to change."

"That's just it. The world must tire of hearing 'Yale Knows Best.' This place has all the answers. Lots of opinions. Little open-mindedness. And Yale does nothing—absolutely nothing—for your spirit. It's sad, isn't it? A great university with ideas about everything, except about what makes life worth living."

We sat silent. "What will you do after college, Doug?"

"Don't know. Grab a pro basketball contract."

We laughed. From sex to cinema to law, Doug's mind might bound. But his body dawdled. We let him walk a bit, rather than dribble, in our basketball games.

"And you?" he asked. "You'll run for office, I suppose."

"Can't say. Right now, I mostly look back. Some nights, I just want to do college all over. Then I think, why, everyone must want to do that. And probably, being who we are, we'd do it over the same way."

"I wonder," he shrugged. "One thing I'd like to do differently. I'd like to be in the Glee Club."

I looked at him, and he at me. I wanted, suddenly, to know him better. This cause and that commitment had prevented it. Now there was no time. Before us lay a journey into age without youth. He was a classmate I met at some past, dusty crossroad; there we spoke a bit, in soft tones and sad. Two students, dawn born, noon acquainted, bundling our feelings over our shoulders, and wistfully sauntering down our separate paths.

Doug always made me wonder whether I'd made the friends I should have. Back then many of us stuck tightly to our own social or political circles. That failing was mine, not Yale's, and not the 1960s. George Pataki, who went on to become a three-term governor of New York, and I were in the Political Union. We worked together on Union campus campaigns and George reached out, but we were never truly close. Dang it, George was just not polished. He was a mailman's son who was raised on a farm where, he later wrote, "the hard joke was that each year our best crop was rocks." And Yale had admitted sons of immigrants who had never completed high school, but whom Kingman Brewster and his admissions director, Inky Clark, to their real credit, had helped to attend a great university. Some gulfs back then were a bit wide for lots of us—especially for a somewhat priggish fellow like myself—to fully cross. Is there no time left to know the classmates we never really knew? Is it not possible after all these years to stand on one shore of the decade that has been our Great Divide and see across the waters? Maybe now some healing conversations can be had on the origins of our opportunities and the seeds of our discords—or has the legacy of the Sixties defied even the softening of time and made it too difficult for that?

My own path has brought me back to Yale only infrequently. But in a sense there is no need to return. Yale is, in fact, a state of mind: you leave Yale, but it never leaves you.

I wonder sometimes if what happened to me at college was because of Yale or because of the decade I went there. Whatever the answer, those years were never carefree.

Do I pin too much blame on the Sixties? It's a fair question. It's not that the education wars all began in the 1960s: witness the gallant but pitiful attempt of William Jennings Bryan in the notorious 1925 Scopes Monkey Trial to keep the teaching of evolution out of Tennessee public schools. Because education is important, it has and always will be controversial; it's just that during the Sixties the controversy was given a razor's edge. After the harsh campus clashes of the decade, education became a political battleground in a way it had never been before. Right and left bend education to their ends. Today's textbook wars, the righteous legions out to ban the teaching of evolution and other scientific "heresies," the curriculum standoffs between Western Civilization courses and courses in other cultures, the temptations of accrediting agencies to impose their policy preferences upon the process, all attest to the ongoing feuds. The champions of No Child Left Behind and Common Core have worthwhile aims, but they face deep wellsprings of distrust. It is not just the old American suspicion of centralized government, now corporeally embodied in the Department of Education. The advocates of school vouchers and choice and home schooling fear an ideological crusade too. And during the Sixties education did in fact become infused with an ideology that continues to mistake the adoption of agendas with the acquisition of knowledge as it pursues the impossible dream of incontestable truth.

Parents for many reasons are on the lookout these days. I know I was. It came to my attention that no small part of my son's eighth-grade American history class was devoted to the bashing of the imperialist pretensions of James K. Polk, the bellicosity of Theodore Roosevelt, and the toxic racism of Woodrow Wilson, three deeply flawed presidents who nonetheless accomplished some very meaningful and significant things. So I determined to get to know the teacher, whom I found to be one of the most caring and inspiring my son ever had. But inspiration with a little balance, please, the kind of conversation I always wish I'd had at Yale with John Morton Blum.

Is balance a pipe dream? Education in the 1960s was less about inquiry than about engagement. I am tempted even now to feel deeply shortchanged. But not entirely. The sheer intensity of fifty years ago will not—and should not—go away. Whenever I take a comfortable view of the world or a self-satisfied look at my own existence, my memories of Yale intervene to remind me of my eternally sheltered state. How can you feel content when others are not? Back then college constantly asked that question, which is one Americans should always want to answer.

Have I sought an answer? Not hard enough—no one ever does. But one measure of the impact of the Sixties is that Americans are now no strangers to guilt—our consciences have begun to link up with our brains. Conservatives who talk of enterprise zones as a way to revive the inner city and of school vouchers as a means of empowering the poor don't acknowledge our debt to the 1960s—the decade we love to hate. That student with whom I occasionally pitched football ran for president in 2000 on a platform of compassionate conservatism. Many saw that as a contradiction in terms and say he never once sought to practice it. But the fellow whom I thought so oblivious to the entire decade showcased a slogan that maybe, just maybe, owes something to his years at Yale.

In 1967, Bill Hilgendorf died. He slipped while climbing mountains outside Hong Kong and fell to his death. Bill was our class president at Yale, and he had an even manner that was welcome, especially given the times. In the 1960s, there was always the temptation to draw some larger lesson from everything, but Bill's death was just immensely sad, a single tragic accident. It is right that we mourn our leaders, whether of a class or a nation. Years later, I went to the Capitol to stand in silence as President Reagan lay in state. I had served in his administration, so my gratitude, particularly at that time, was profound. Resisting the urge to contextualize has become harder since the Sixties; it's more difficult to take life as it comes, to see events and people simply for themselves. But to my relief, I never tried to place President Reagan's death in the social and political battles of the time. His death became, like Bill's, an individual act of taking leave, on its own terms immensely sad.

I remember my reaction because moments for their own sake were becoming more unusual. One can respect the real accomplishments of the Sixties and still know that the decade's sum of campus rancor was nothing less than tragic. America today is beset by animosity. When the partisan barricades are manned by mortal enemies, when indictments and impeachments become increasingly the means of resolving our differences, when "me" and "my" transcend "us" as a country, it is impossible to think that all is well. When we survey the harsh, mistrustful culture that destroys the remnants of our sense of community, it is impossible not to see the seeds of incivility that were planted in the 1960s. The pseudo-education that preached but one right and moral view was quick to brand all others as not just incorrect but illegitimate, which brings listening to an end.

As a boy, I would sometimes curl up in a chair in the evening and read Jules Verne, the nineteenth-century French science fiction writer, or George Orwell, the prophetic British novelist. I used to dub this my goose-pimple hour, because it left me so very chilly about what the future held for me. We now have no shortage of futurists predicting everything from the coming of nirvana or, more likely, the last man on earth, or everything in between. The futurists have their place, but even the best of them are unconvincing, because the pace of change and the exciting and terrifying world of tomorrow are quite impossible to comprehend. Once upon a time, I thought Frankenstein beyond the realm of possibility. But what if, muses *Washington Post* columnist Michael Gerson, there emerges an "artificial intelligence that becomes superior to human intelligence and annoyed by human existence." Or what if, he continues, "the splicing of genes could eventually become a do-it-yourself technology, allowing the creation of some deliberately species-ending virus." Or what if . . . The Bomb. Who knows?

People ask: "Aren't you glad you were born when you were?" Or: "Don't you dread the world that awaits our grandchildren?" But I'll never answer either question "Yes," because what matters is that American institutions, government and business, medical and scientific, military and media, humanitarian and educational (K through doctorate), be prepared to meet whatever comes. And that must mean the academic diatribes and animosities that engender overblown symbolic spats be seen for what they are. What we need to do is ensure humanity's survival. A campus in a Sixties mood is not best equipped for that.

The close-minded campus atmosphere has long survived the decade that principally gave it birth. Charlottesville,

Virginia, is a special place to live, but at election time the
yard signs and bumper stickers play in unison as if under the
baton of a great conductor. When Cambridge, Charlottesville, Madison, Berkeley, or Chapel Hill return such lopsided
majorities for the most liberal candidates, it does not mean
that university towns are somehow wrong, only shockingly
short of dissonant voices. To challenge the prevailing dogmas today requires courage, a commodity that educational
bureaucracies and campus thought-police endeavor to keep
in short supply. Controversial speakers are lucky if their campus reception is merely rude: George W. Bush's Secretary of
State Condoleezza Rice felt compelled to withdraw from a
2014 commencement address at Rutgers University after students sat outside the president's office and shouted "Cancel
Condi" at him as he emerged from meetings.

The phenomenon is epidemic. A 2014 Campus Disinvitation Report prepared by the Foundation for Individual
Rights in Education estimates that since 2000 there have
been fifty-seven instances in which a speaker was disinvited,
nineteen instances in which a speaker backed out in the face
of protest, twelve instances in which a speaker was repeatedly
disrupted, and 114 instances in which the disinvitation effort
fell short. Anytime anyone says anything displeasing to anybody there is a danger, or so it seems, of having the campus
welcome mat withdrawn.

Even being a defender of free speech can make one a target. At Yale in the fall of 2015 a professor offering a measured
case for respectful dialogue was shouted down: "You should
not sleep at night! You are disgusting." And at the University
of Missouri, an ESPN reporter, Tim Tai, was turned on by a
crowd that included, of all people, university staff and an assistant professor of mass media, who called out, "Who wants

to help me get this reporter out of here? I need some muscle over here."

It's an old Sixties story gathering new momentum as sensitivities give rise to codes and zones of censorship and as commencement speakers become more and more a fraternity of the bland. Even Halloween costumes, long a source of social parody and expressive abandon, have lately come under the assault of campus sensitivity. (Not to worry: Although costumes featuring cultural stereotypes are newly risky, dressing as a Starbucks cup may still be safe.) Countering offensive speech is our First Amendment right and social obligation. Prohibiting it is no one's prerogative. Yet the line between criticism of opposing views and suppression of them is becoming ever less distinct. It's not just political and religious conservatives who feel the campus lash. Those who engineered the fall of Harvard President Larry Summers swear he was his own worst enemy, and that a more diplomatic leader could have accomplished much of what he tried to do. All true, but anyone who came of age in the Sixties knew Summers was riding a beast. There are things one dare not mention, minefields one dare not enter, topics not up for discussion, subjects one dare not broach. Summers did, and it was only a matter of time until the end.

In the smug little world of the Ivies, Yale graduates have to be careful what we say about our Cambridge friends. So rest assured that if I ever hear the phrase "pointy-headed Harvard intellectual" again, I shall despair. I don't really know what this phrase even means. I should be grateful, however, if some very pointy-headed intellectual develops a cure for my rheumatoid arthritis. Smarts of every personal description would seem to be the goal.

The drumbeat of anti-intellectualism now serves to distract from such real college crises as lessened courage on the part of those who nominally lead them. The vanguard of the Sixties, the ironically named SDS—Students for a "Democratic" Society—pioneered the techniques of intimidating college administrations: grabbing microphones, shouting down speakers, occupying administration buildings, forcing classes to be cancelled, with the greatest casualty of all again being unapologetic speech. In 2014, the president of the University of Iowa apologized for making the perfectly honest statement that "human nature" might realistically impede the highly desirable goal of eliminating every last campus sexual assault. The president of Smith College felt compelled to apologize for stating, ecumenically, that "all lives matter" in the wake of the tragic Ferguson, Missouri, shooting of a black teenager by a town police officer. The result of all this is a loss of true and resonant voices for the values of the great enterprise of higher learning. The Sixties sought such shrinkage. How small these words that now tremble at themselves and this language that is fearful of its shadow.

It will hardly do for me to acknowledge my occasional uneasiness in the 1960s as a white Southerner at Yale and to overlook the greater discomfort black students may feel there today. Slights and unwelcoming gestures are somehow forever flying beneath the radar, and I do not doubt that the hurt visited is real. But the answer cannot be forsaking the foundational principles of free expression or quailing before the most immediate stimuli or cultivating the language of apology (Yale President Peter Salovey, "We failed you"; resigning University of Missouri President Tim Wolfe, "I am sorry, and my apology is long overdue"; Yale Silliman College Master Nicholas Christakis, "I'm genuinely sorry . . . to have disappointed you. I've disappointed myself."). Not a word about whether the endless presentation of demands ("mandatory cultural competency training" for all staff and faculty) and the search for separate spaces, white and black, are inhibiting the gifts that persons of every color might bring to the universities of which they now are part. Not a mention of the joy the Sixties and their sense of grievance stole from students then and threaten to take now. It's enough to make me grab my beat-up megaphone and holler forth to future generations that life is not all grim, that one does not betray a cause by embracing the beauty of a moment, that the Sixties have no right to deprive you, as they did us, of the exuberance of living and the joy of learning too.

I care, because I was myself a professor for some years at the University of Virginia Law School. Teaching is hard work if you don't place yourself on cruise control and if you ask not only the good what, when, and where questions but also the continually probing whys. Every teacher knows that there are days when a class just seems to jell and come together, and days when it's all flat, leaving you feeling empty and second-guessing yourself for hours. I had my share of both, but I remember still the enlivened faces of my students when divergent points of view were respected and encouraged. You learn a lot from students then, and it makes you happy to be alive.

But learning depends on the willingness to ask hard questions. I admit I too seldom ask such questions of myself. So it's understandable, I suppose, if institutions lose the ability to pose hard questions to themselves. To wit: Are students reluctant to voice their views because they fear bad grades? Are junior faculty afraid to speak their convictions because they fear not getting tenure? Are administrations aware of how their school's suppressive antics play in the eyes of the

American public? The most difficult question of all, though,
is how the ability to ask hard questions comes to be lost. Did
the climate of the 1960s impart respectability to intolerance
such that academic self-examination becomes less frequent
and introspection more a futile exercise?

What good comes to society from academic insularity?
What good comes to universities when bad taste, whatever
that may mean, lies outside the ambit of free speech? The
First Amendment is a universal friend: Racial minorities have
used the power of words and peaceful protest to effect enormous change throughout this country's history. How sad to
now find the Great Amendment taking sides. Groupthink in
great universities depresses free speech, because the business
of academia, unlike, say, dentistry, is to debate and amplify
ideas. Diversity of viewpoint is at least a modest hedge against
monumental error and unintended consequences, the dangers
of which rise with the complexity of life around us. Environ-
mental crises, world population growth, bioethical dilemmas,
technology's promises and problems, the preservation of liberty in an era of unprecedented global danger would all seem
to demand universities whose fealty to diverse discussion inspires public confidence. Their imbalance is unworthy of a
great profession, one whose teaching and research has helped
as much as anything to make America what it is.

The point must not be overstated, or every fringe silliness
exaggerated. Some fields of study are far more radicalized
than others. Every school has its Chipping, every university
its hidden jewels, teachers who touch generations of students
with their wisdom and insight. The University of Colorado
caused something of a stir recently when it took the baby step
of bringing in a "visiting scholar in conservative thought and
policy" to begin to redress the imbalance in its faculty. For-

tunately, the guinea pig for the experiment, Professor Steven
Hayward, declined to act like a curiosity: "[E]ven a conser-
vative professor who feels like a Soviet dissident on today's
campuses ought to uphold the traditional model of teaching
by presenting a full spectrum of views in the classroom, rather
than engage in counter-indoctrination."

Sadly, in its closed-mindedness the campus is not alone.
The anger nurtured in the Sixties has its remissions, but
stands ever at the ready for the next right cause. Now our
national leaders are picking up the cudgels of debate with
deadly seriousness, with all the venom and vehemence the
Sixties brought into fashion. Perhaps our generation may still
wish to say good riddance to the good times students spent
before we went to college. Perhaps a glare was as good as a
smile. But what we in the Sixties saw as privileged laughter
should have been allowed to play the smallest part in building
bonds of respect and cords of camaraderie among the future
leaders of our country. For all our education, that was a lesson never learned.

It hurts, because all the intolerance in which my university engaged has never managed to extinguish all affection. It
hurts, because our generation had such great potential. Yale
in the 1960s reflected that potential as no other place. Future
presidents, vice presidents, senators, CEOs, judges, artists,
writers, academics, journalists, ambassadors, and diplomats
were part of the cornucopia of that place, and the brightest
minds had gathered there to teach them.

But how Yale taught us was another question. We were
given license to place law, science, humanities, and the arts
at the service of politics and ideology. It became more ac-
ceptable in that era to bend the rigors of professional discipline to a preconceived, political result. It became more

difficult to regard inquiry as disinterested, dialogue as open, or knowledge as so much as a semi-pure state. Education was subverted to reflect the fevers of that time and place and to forsake the longer view. Yale of all places should have stood against these trends. Instead, it succumbed to them. The tragedy of it all was that Yale had—and has—so very much to offer. Only such a magnificent institution could have forfeited such an unparalleled chance and opportunity, but that is what my college in the 1960s did.

So our graduation came and went, a graduation into a society Yale had taught us to condemn. There were speeches, intonations, the usual stones of discontent. At the end, we shook hands and smiled. Few shouts of joy, fewer tasseled hats sailing proud into the sky. It was not a time to act carefree, as though we knew nothing of affliction. The occasion, someone said, impressed as wise beyond its years. Maybe some good would one day come of it all. I'll always be a Yale alumnus; I'll always contribute my fair share. But back then, the songs had ceased. The shortest, gladdest years of life were melodies long gone.

II. The Destruction of Commitment

FATHER CROUCHED on the outermost edge of his chair, one hand on his knee, the other with forefinger wagging, his voice grave, his short frame thrust forward, his whole body coiled for emphasis. "Never," he said, shooting me the straightest stare I ever remember, "never let your father learn of your indulgence. Never let me learn, even once, that it has gotten the better of you."

"It," of course, was unmentionable. "It" was set to snare with social shame, bodily sores, and irons of forced wedlock those fool enough to venture near. "It's a car with no brakes. Don't you ever start it up, son."

"Son" was Father's way of meaning business. "Son" impressed on my young brain the endless weight of family probity. It connoted consequences of unspeakable unpleasantness. The world might mellow, but not Father, whose morality was like a spear some ancient, upright king flung to the ground, and which struck and stood ever since, steadfast and unquivering.

He galloped over the long evening, trampling all excuses.

"It matters not what your friends do. I do not hold them ac-
countable.

"It is never safe; beware the woman who swears it is.

"You are not in love. Love, unlike lust, does not degrade
its object.

"You are not like the swine in your uncle's barnyard. You
are a young man of duty—to myself, to your dear mother, to
your future wife and children whom, though you may not
know it, your own manhood from this second will set the
example.

"Have I made myself clear?"

"Yes sir."

And he departed.

Father never again addressed the subject. He permitted
himself one terrifying thrust into consciousness, after which
all matters he deemed delicate bolted shut.

It wasn't just Father. The 1950s left no doubt that sex
was the enemy. It ranked right up there with communism
as something to watch out for. Physical charm was poison
ivy. A woman was a vase I dare not touch. Eyes prowled me
when I was around women, as they did in museums. Society
conspired to make of conscience a chaperon, to place me
in the care of some ever-frowning portrait, some doughty
model of continence whose eyes sobered at the very recollection of temptation and whose renown rested on eternal will.

It was all so unnecessary. I was such a shy boy, around
girls anyway. I knew I was supposed to act differently around
them, but nothing more than that. I had no sister. I was quite
safely refrigerated from the opposite sex. I went to an all-
male school, St. Christopher's, whose companion, St. Cath-
erine's, was only several blocks away but might as well have
been in England. Boys and girls from the two schools did not
even make each other's acquaintance until Miss Donnan's

sixth-grade cotillion (my parents insisted sixth grade was too early and held me back until the seventh). Miss Donnan's was a large, rectangular, scrupulously regular room, suffocated by light, consecrated to forced pairings, padded with "instructors" pinning commendations on their charges, directed by Miss Donnan in tuneful cadence from her platform.

It was also, to its last varnished inch, the sanctioned setting. Richmond, Virginia, evoked powdered wigs and silver buckles, its life a minuet between the sexes. There were gallant pleas and silken phrases, all manner of "May I's" and "By all manses," mazes of shapes, forms, and sizes to which it was important to be fitted early. Father took it seriously. Ceremony, he explained, lay like "some timeless social oath," there for "generations of gentlemen to swear upon." Manners fortified man against his nature, gave him a gentle mien, tried to shape a thing of grace from unconscionably vulgar raw material. But ceremony had to be mastered and made comfortable, until which time it baffled and confounded. Yet there was a constant youthful restlessness to which even Miss Donnan's genuflected. For every so often, at the very end of an evening, a rustle of excitement came over the dance hall, and Miss Donnan announced a "free round," a chance actually to choose one's own partner.

"Would you like to dance?" I asked, having watched the girl and pondered the question all evening.

She sat silent.

"That's all right. I could ask you another evening, that is, if you're not feeling well."

A slight smile, and a blush. Now my knees were knocking too hard to dance, so I said, "May I get you some lemonade?"

My night was pure bliss when she nodded.

• • •

All this ritual in Richmond pointed toward one inevitable end. If you hear the 1950s was all about Hound Dog, don't believe it. Marriage was the thing. The jump from Miss to Mrs. was thought to be a great accomplishment (though many who most influenced me had never taken the leap). It was a failure for a girl to earn a diploma before winning a ring. Marriage meant respectability, because from it followed children, a home, and all good things. These conventions of life would soon enrage the nonconformists of the Sixties, in whose eyes the tedium of bourgeois institutions was a sin. But constancy could be a comfort—or so it seemed back then.

My parents had a wonderful marriage, although it was in no sense a modern one. Father treasured his dinner table, where he sat at one end, Mother at the other, with that long plane of mahogany in between. Father came to Saturday breakfast in his coat and tie. "I do it for your mother," he always said.

Love was not on display before offspring. Father simply left us to deduce it from respect. The strength of his passion was the strength of his respect: never a coarse word to her, never a rude gesture, never a slovenly habit—*never* in all those years.

It would have been unthinkable for Father to stroll our gardens, to learn the names and seasons of our flowers, to remark on the robins that perched daily on our lawn. Mother alone was permitted to release him from manhood—he learned, in time, to accept the extravagant beauty in his midst because, he said, "it gives her such pleasure." If she marveled at a sunrise, so could he. If she laughed at children's nonsense, so could he. But not until. In a time that struck men senseless, she gave him back his sight.

It would have been unbecoming in those days for Mother to pursue a profession. To discuss finances would have been as inappropriate as indulging in brandy or cigars. So she learned to listen, to use humor, and to make Father talk the more. She took up books and gardens, tennis and travel, and service to the poor. In a time that stole independence from women, he gave her the chance for stimulating interests and for friends.

How much the meaning of marriage is ever glimpsed by children, I cannot say. Marriage had, as always, its surface of minutiae in which I was quite consumed. Mother fixed my lunch; Father supervised my homework. Mother made me clean my room; Father made me weed the sidewalk. Mother made me write fifty times the proper code of behavior; Father just took off his belt. Mother was someone with whom to bicker—so long as she didn't threaten to tell Father. And so it went. I was so absorbed relating to each of them that I never understood, until much later, how deeply they related to each other.

Things were pretty much the same back then, and that sameness in itself was comforting and good. As life unfolded in warm and reassuring rhythms, it became easy to believe the 1950s were as wonderful for everyone as they were for Mom and Dad and me. When threats of polio and H-bombs made things seem pretty scary, marriage and family would step in to make life stable and secure. Yet all the formality of Richmond touched outer lives, not inner beings. In fact, the worldview of the 1950s saw intimate selves as threats. The family values of that decade brought happiness to many, but family values weren't so sweet for spouses trapped in soulless unions—those whom the specter of social disapproval condemned to desperately respectable days. What the tribunes of righteousness missed then as now is that one can lead a life of perfect rectitude and be as lonely as can be.

I never sensed that growing up. And even living in the

1950s could not shield me from adolescence. When I was fourteen years old, I began gingerly to sin. Girls were to blame, for girls required style. Most of my friends knew how to dress, how to light up, how to cast cool glances, how to do funny little flips from diving boards that guaranteed the girls would notice. A corner drugstore—Doc White's—had become our commons. There we preened on a thick carpet of candy wrappers, cigarette butts, and crushed paper cups. Our chatter ran endlessly to parties thrown in the basements of our parents' homes—basements, of course, off-limits to parents. There lights flashed off and pop hits piled atop the phonograph. Dancing became "slow dancing"—cheek to cheek.

It was not destined to last. At fourteen I made my fatal mistake—a Tuesday evening television program called *The Bob Cummings Show*. To borrow a line from *Oklahoma!*, that show went about as far as it could go. Its hero was a crew-cut photographer with a lecherous laugh, a disapproving shrew of an assistant, and an inventory of shapely models on whom Cummings lavished the most captivating repertoire of lines and moves. Each model was made to feel absolutely delicious in her perfect pose. The TV, unfortunately, had to be turned way down so Cummings's laughs—and the models' squeals—wouldn't reach Father's study upstairs. Alas, Cummings did not forever escape detection, and the discovery moved Father to act.

I was promptly shipped to boarding school—the Lawrenceville School in Lawrenceville, New Jersey, where academics were strict and social life was severely regulated. To say there was social life at Lawrenceville may be hyperbole. There was a spring prom, where pictures of our dates were published in a special edition of the school newspaper, and there were Tea Dances in the various Circle Houses, where a flock of girls arrived from schools near Trenton late Saturday afternoon and departed early Saturday evening.

There was also a less structured sociability, not featured, like the Tea Dances, in the school catalogue. My senior year, several classmates would slip into New York for what they said were their "appointments." There was always some feigned disinclination to discuss particulars with younger cubs, until one day, one of them hit the jackpot and contracted gonorrhea. He was roaming the halls, raving on about it, burnishing his ultimate status in a school where I, for one, began to tremble at the thought of suspect toilet seats. Perhaps some others had the same fear. No one dared voice it, and thus donate himself to lasting ridicule. I was left to slink quietly to a different bathroom and, even there, scrub the skin off the latrine.

For the most part, however, things continued on their conventional course. Relations between the sexes were so stylized in my teenage years that I was almost bound to develop an overactive imagination. Whether others did, I cannot say, but I find it hard to believe their minds were any more content than mine with the choreographed courtships laid out for them. Fantasies are part of all teenagers' lives, but the restrictive realities of the Fifties sure set my thoughts adrift.

My mind ran everywhere—I would rummage through literary heroines like old toys in a closet, picking one, making believe she was my mate, and then toss her over my shoulder, digging on for the next. Scarlett O'Hara was my early favorite, but she grew too spiteful for even an imaginary courtship, so I switched to Elizabeth Bennet and Jane Eyre, passionate women of insight—the kind who, one day, in spite of myself, would discover something there.

Soon I sought women of my own imagining, called up, cast off in endless visual variety: Nell, a lithe and supple harvester in some distant firmament of wheat, whom I hoisted upward and upward, coaxing forth all her native sparkle and wit; or Suzanne, a pert lass, with short blonde hair, a Scottish kilt, cream-skinned, whose eyes in spring were a cool rosé—I saw us lunching alone in the Highlands.

Sex wasn't absent from the Fifties, only more solitary and less visible. We were each left to decorate our inner chambers. I would shut my door, pull down the shades, close my eyes, and listen to music by the hour. Here, at last, I was out of range and at peace. With music, the awkwardness fell from me. I became loose, a magician of mood—of sunny, warm embraces, of cold, starlit longings, of swift, chugging trains like the "Old 97," and of slow, sublime rivers like the lovely Shenandoah. The song was my chariot, whisking women I wanted to places I alone could go. Before sleep, I would dream of strumming my soul out one enraptured evening, there beneath the balcony, to the girl of my dreams, on whose finger the diamond would sparkle forever.

Real life was seldom romantic. In June, I left Lawrenceville for Richmond, where nothing between the sexes would be left to informality or chance. Summers at home were scheduled tight—a long queue of black-tie galas—Mother forwarded the invitations even before I began my final exams. There were luncheons in the day and debutante parties every evening, sometimes on sloped lawns, more often at The Commonwealth Club or The Country Club of Virginia. I went, because my parents' friends were always hosting these parties, and Mother insisted, "no questions, dear," that I attend.

If they kept us continually at parties, nothing would happen in the backseat of the car. The affairs warmed up by ten o'clock and disbanded after breakfast at one-thirty, not the ideal booster for next morning's employment. They were outpourings of unabashed affluence, small dowries showered on drink and arresting appetizers, bands and bubbly fountains, mood lighting and theme setting—nothing too grand for a daughter's big debut. The best of them were exquisite, if one came prepared to distinguish between the decorativeness and the Luddites on whom it was lavished. Myself, for one. I was still clumsy at small talk. I just stood around with my frozen smile, while my legs ached and suspenders bit into my shoulders. Beside me my debutante date, a blithe, aromatic creature peacocked in her evening dress, standing there with her frozen smile. We had exhausted the pleasantries driving to the dance, and there remained nothing of conversation to sustain us through the evening. Then some guy wandered over to her and shouted above the band to talk:

"Great to see you again."

"Fine, how about yourself?"

"Thank you. What are you doing this summer?"

"Filing and typing. That sort of thing."

"Great! Really is. Wish I could get a job like that."

"Filing?"

"Sorry, thought you said FLYING. Stewardess and all that."

"No, filing."

"Magnificent! Terrific! Really envy you, Gladys. Say, did I see you at Diane's the other night?"

The band would not permit an answer.

It is easy enough to poke fun at Richmond, Virginia, in the days before the sexual revolution. The city was in some respects a stodgy place where social conventions kept sexual disruptions to a minimum. The modern word for it, I suppose, is repression. Richmond understood, however, the meaning that social support imparted to personal relationships. And it knew the value that longevity imparted to commitment. Those were insights that the 1960s soon brought into question.

At eighteen, I arrived at Yale, my third all-male institution. Like St. Christopher's and Lawrenceville, Yale seemed unhinged by thoughts of frequent gender interaction. Women at Yale were something of a side dish, the main course being, of course, male bonding. In classes, sports, activities, societies—women were forbidden. They were reduced to weekend fare, bused in wholesale from, say, Vassar to Saturday socials known as "mixers." For at least the first half hour, no mixer ever lived up to its name. The room wore a homely, obligatory cast (those who were "with it" in college needed no mixer to mix in). Men milled on one side, women on the other, until some smart buck figured "mixer" didn't mean with his roommate, and that by invading the other herd first, he might haul something choice in.

But elsewhere the times were not so staid as the mixer might have indicated. I read somewhere that a young man who spent his apprenticeship wading nude with two women into the ocean at San Francisco's Aquatic Park had founded the New York City League for Sexual Freedom. Quickly free-love chapters sprouted at U.C.L.A., Stanford, and the University of Texas. "Do I want it? Does it hurt anyone else?" were to be the sole prerequisites. The cause was cheered as an epic American insurrection. "Man," shouted the manifestos, "will only become free when he can overcome his own guilt and when society stops trying to manage his sex life for him."

It's not that free love or nudist camps swept the country. They didn't, but the shock value of such things suddenly made the Fifties seem so very uninspired. During the Sixties we were intent on injecting excitement into every cranny of our lives. The new sin was being dull. Before the Sixties, dullness could actually be a good thing. It meant solidity and dependability, the kind of qualities that went into making a good citizen. If a man was dull, why, he was probably a good provider and parent and worker and churchgoer. But along with dismissing the bigoted, blue-collar hard-hats, the so-phisticates of the Sixties had no use for the middle-class clod whose drab routine filled his string of dreary days. Home to work and back again was not the way to spend one's life. Check any bar or nightclub and you'll know this disapproval of dullness is here to stay. Most of us still fret about living dull lives—same job, same city—sameness with no spice.

Above all, we discovered in the Sixties that our lives were sexually dull. The dullness was apparent in our apparel: for women, the apron; for men, the gray suit. Natural in-stincts had been repressed by two different sets of ancestors, the Victorians and the Puritans. The Victorians imparted an elaborate set of external rules; the Puritans instilled a sense of internal guilt. The culture was thus full of frustrations and hang-ups that no one could explain or dared express. At the dead center of all the dullness was monogamy itself. Families were the most sexually confining of settings—All American portraits of sexual repression or indifference.

The Sixties determined to brighten this bleak landscape. The decade was a giant unveiling. Hugh Hefner uncovered women physically, as Alfred Kinsey had uncovered all of us statistically. Nudity seemed a wholesome attempt to banish the dark lagoon of shameful thoughts. Sexual freedom was sought, as Ponce de León had sought the fountain of youth. Gay Talese wrote that "alternate-life-style communities were

finally coming of age in America. . . . There were now [by
1970] in the nation approximately two thousand separate set-
tlements of various sizes and distinctions." One of the most
upscale was the Sandstone Retreat, with a "large membership
of stable couples, young middle-class sensualists who believed
that their personal relationships would be enhanced, rather
than shattered, by the elimination of sexual possessiveness."

Pretty soon, we were on a roll. Sex was the discovery of
the Sixties. All hail, open air; lance the boil of guilt! Ogle the
suntanned leg on GM's finest. Spy the skin on every news-
stand, screen, and billboard. Hear the dons of science bark
safer, simpler ways to stop conception. Listen, the ethicists
say feelings are what count. Read statistics on each minutia
of erotic movement; see a depiction of every nuance in tech-
nique. Rise to the liberating sun of sexual revolution; wake
to the banishment of the long Victorian night. What prayer
do parents have against the pill and penicillin, or against a
booming *Playboy*, itself a patriarch, but of sex as pop culture?
So why, Father, why? Why obsolesce me? I should be a stalwart son, indeed, to resist an urge so free.

When popular culture starts to turn, no moment is exempt. For my friend Jerry, Sunday was a wasted evening, one
he reserved for lying on a couch and recounting his exploits.
It grated—him relating, me listening like some child habitu-
ally read to before bedtime, him polishing his coveted keys
to love's portals, him flourishing the superiority of spending
weekends his way. "Knock it off, Jerry!" I yelled, when I
could stand it no longer. "Leave!"

Jerry only laughed. "Why should I! What's to be ashamed
of? Shame is their stake through your soul. Who's driving
it? Old people. Old people wishin' they could rev it up
too. Old people whose glands lie rotting in their trousers.

C'mon, Wilk. You're the youngest old fart I know. Just look at them. Behind every prudish mask, someone's retching green with envy."

"Maybe. Maybe they've just learned and got it right."

"C'mon. She wants to. You want to. What's the hitch?"

"Women, dammit. They don't waltz away from bed the way you do from gin rummy. How do you implore Debbie one minute, ignore her the next?"

"So that's it. She who lays you loves you. Who gave you the line on women? Treat them as adults, why don't you? Women do grow up, you know. Make their choices, take their chances. I can't believe you," he roared. "What a funky little prude for a friend!"

It would have been nice, occasionally, to have had a tale of my own. Jerry's were real enough. Whether Jerry was for real, I could not say. Neither, perhaps, could he. The person and the pose seemed to merge, and to suit him.

The New Morality seemed made with Jerry in mind. He had, he always said, timed puberty just right. The Sixties, he thought, were his kind of day. Society was sweet, he chuckled, to want to limit sex to marriage, but marriage was too cramped a chamber for something so combustible, like "catching a bee in your bare hand." Once marriage might have worked, but not now, "when people buzz about the way they do today." Besides, the pill and the pull were here and now, and marriage was a long way off—after college, the draft, and grad school. No one expected us to wait. "Look," he said one evening, "there's a bitchy little war out there that could spoil all the parties. Who've you ever humped, Wilk? Wanna go to your grave in Vietnam a virgin?"

Jerry wore the sunny countenance of a contemporary man. The world stood by his side. Society was more tolerant, the self more its own guide. And there was Jerry surfing in on all those waves, tanned and dauntless, whooping his lusty YEEOWs. If there was something selfish about Jerry's presence on the surf, there was something so joyous, so open, so enviable about his ride. From the shore I watched him, without compass, not knowing what I thought or why. Was it not nobler to be bold and wrong, than too unsteady to attempt the ride? What antichrist had come and made me ask such questions? "Hey, that's the trouble, you question too much," Jerry chuckled. "What's that they say: 'Don't fret it. Let it.'" And the next wave came rolling in.

I think back on Jerry often. His sexual surfing was not so unusual. Ours was the generation that couldn't sit still. We moved to new liaisons the way we moved to new causes. When I chide my kids about their limited attention spans, when screens click back and forth before me, it's not much different from the ceaseless motions of my youth. I had to run hard to catch up with the Sixties. Being "with it" wasn't easy for someone of my background. But Lord, how I tried.

My junior year, I began seeing someone steadily. One spring weekend, I asked her to Yale. Though weekend hotel rates in New Haven were confiscatory (it was just before the day of competition from the dormitories), I booked her a room, and things seemed set. Friday night, we had one of those good lobster-bib dinners. Saturday, we moseyed about New Haven in the morning and watched a tennis match that afternoon. Saturday evening, we had tickets to a play. May the actors forgive my inattention. I sat there the whole evening, plotting my next move.

The weekend had gone well. I wanted to go to her room. I also knew it was expected. Saturday night was the jackpot for guys who had shown gals a good time. If a Yalie didn't score on Saturday evening, either he didn't care for his date or there was no moxie in him. And, of course, I had to face Jerry on Sunday evening. So I walked into her room, turned on a lamp (not the bright ceiling light), took off my coat, kicked off my loafers, and sat down, rather casually, on the bed. For a long moment, I wondered what she would do. The room had a chair, her perfect refusal. She stepped into the bathroom, came back, stared for a minute at the chair, and then walked over and sat on the bed. Not aggressive, but nice. My heart pounded. I talked idly, kissed her, and reached to unbutton her blouse.

Something happened. I felt clammy. My movement was jerky, set loose from my head. I feared she would find me awkward, an amateur. But it was more than that. The room seemed suddenly less private, with two great intruders, Father's eyes. He was there. He forbade me. I tried but I could not get rid of him, even with this chance—this wonderful relationship—dissolving right before my eyes. My hands grew flustered. My desire dwindled. My sensual being belonged to some huge colony where Father's brand burned deep into millions, beating mercilessly down on nonconforming spirits, a stern, omniscient sun.

I did not apologize; I did not explain. Something crisp about "upbringing" was all I said. She seemed to understand, to the extent one can ever understand behavior so abrupt and strange. What she wished to know, I could not say, too distraught within myself to let it outside. I had tried and failed. I had, I knew, made my leap for sexual freedom and plunged down, ever down, until darkness purged my eyes of envy for this wild, unchastened age. There would be no more questions, no more conflicts, no more doubts—only labor of the long, straight line. Protest was useless; I put on my shoes and coat and left.

So there I was, trapped between past and present. One

moment a product of my upbringing, the next, attempting a flight away from it. Father was fearsome, but the culture of the Sixties had this way of bearing down on you until you gave up and believed. Sex became the Sixties thing, as marriage had been the foremost Fifties institution.

Marriage took a pounding during the Sixties, the battering ram being Betty Friedan's book, *The Feminine Mystique*. What Friedan pioneered now seems absolutely right and just: equal pay, maternity leave, child-care centers, and, above all, a role for women in all walks of American life. To make her points, Friedan took on marriage and homemaking and child-rearing in relentless prose. There was more to life than diapers and carpools. The cleaning and the cooking and the laundry and the sewing were now of lesser worth. Confinement in the kitchen led to desperation in the marriage; feminine malaise became, in Friedan's phrase, "the problem that has no name."

Divorce rates doubled between 1965 and 1976; divorce laws became increasingly no-fault. In this sense, a necessary step took place during the Sixties: some unions just cannot be made to work. But the era's standards for personal fulfillment were set so high that any human institution was almost bound to come up short. So it was with marriage, the latest target in the line of the decade's discontents.

Indeed, the monotony of marriage talk was not confined to just one sex. Daily life at home and work was not all glamorous for men, and Friedan's message reached all ears. Our parents' lives seemed duller now, and Friedan more correct than even she supposed.

Some of my classmates even echoed Friedan. Charlie's parents were divorced. They had sought security in marriage, he said, but found a suffocation of the spirit—too much of their early fondness was for the blanket of matrimony where the warmth seemed more important than with whom it would be shared. The blanket, swore Jerry, meant to tame each rising generation, even ours, wild to the last. The blanket, lamented Jim, with which to smother social protest, for what do spouses care?

So marriage came to seem a trip to death in different forms—for Charlie the death of identity, for Jerry the death of freedom, for Jim the death of conscience, for men and women too, the death of romance and of dreams: good-bye to beaches where one might romp, sun, swim, laugh, and drop exhausted on the sand. Farewell to amour by the sea, the feel of tender hands returning, the glimpse of ever in the depth of instant, the peace, the quiet, the easy letdown, in a gull's glide.

All this and more, marriage would demand that I give up! Were the traditional roles of men and women all that we doubted in the Sixties, or was the whole concept of marriage becoming obsolete? In a decade of movement, it seemed commitment could not last. Beauty was in variety, sex being no exception. If there was desperation in the kitchen, why not desperation in bed? Would love not wilt soon enough under routine? How long before the insinuation of selfishness, the unconscious onset of distance, the drowsy cud of habit, the silent molding of emotion, the lazy death of indifference, or perhaps a bicker to the death, the sulking, reproachful, stubborn evenings of the spouses? Was matrimony face creams and flabby paunches, and too few TVs, cars, and telephones? Were its "forevers" unpaid bills, untended children, uncut lawns? What attraction would survive age's burglary of beauty? What vow withstand the sight of grime in bathtubs? What loyalty outlive the lust for different couplings? What love absorb the clash of values, tastes, and aims?

Options and choices for both sexes were rapidly developing, and marriage seemed increasingly for those whose options had run out. I saw a couple who I thought might once have loved each other, but now they sat at dinner across from me, the man obese, unkempt, as though he'd ceased to care, she reading a paper with dead eyes as they ate, not talking except to ask the time. There was no spell to their quiet, just air, as though some coma had long since claimed their marriage as they sat, unblinking, watching love expire.

It had seemed so different. Back home, longevity built bonds. There no desperation; just devotion. I spent many an evening wondering how Mother and Father could make marriage work so well.

After Yale, I attended the University of Virginia School of Law. For a while, women took a backseat to the books. Then, too, female companionship was difficult to come by. The law school in 1968 was nearly an all-male establishment. Each class of three hundred had eight or so women, in whom interest was keen. There was little time to strike out for distant pastures; involvement was an inconvenience law school grades could not afford.

It happened anyway. One Saturday at a football game, a classmate dropped by with his date. He introduced her as Anne, and she sat down between us. He had always spoken so apologetically of her that this meeting caught me up short. I loved the softness of her voice. Her words came carefully, connected beads of thought. She asked about me, how I liked law school, what kind of lawyer I hoped to be. She spoke of mountain life in eastern Tennessee, where she had grown up, of its family bonding, its faith, its beauty, and its hardship. That afternoon she made of conversation a ballet, blending talk with attention, knowing how to engage, how to slip away. Her blonde hair fell on her shoulders, clean, a sylvan waterfall. Instinctively, I touched it, not caring to recall with whom she came. It was awkward to find attraction waxing in a stadium, struck, as if from space, by sonic booms of crowd applause. Whether Harry was rapt in football, or half-hoping to make me a gift of his date, I could not tell. By the second half, Harry and his game had blurred away.

Anne and I saw each other every weekend. Soon I was seeing her during the week, leaving Charlottesville near noon, returning after midnight. We would bolt from her college cafeteria, taking dinner outside, into the hills, wherever we could gaze upon the town. Like most towns in western Virginia, Staunton was well provisioned with churches, Methodist, Baptist, Presbyterian, Protestant to the core. Seen from a distance, it became a village of old steeples, stalwart fingers of godliness, a little town's uplifted prayer. Anne smiled, pristine against the backdrop, a worthy subject for Dutch oils.

"What's your worst nightmare?" she asked one evening.

"Gosh, I don't know that I can pick one. Yes, I can. Growing bald."

"Come. I'm being serious."

"Me too. Growing bald."

"Such male vanity. How am I to cope?"

"Nonsense. Women spend half their lives on their hair. Suppose yours were in danger of dropping out?"

"Is your mother's side bald?" she asked.

"Of course. That's the nightmare."

She was amused, came and settled on my lap and kissed me, then yanked impishly at my hair. "Great subsoil, sweetheart," she laughed. "Looks like tough old growth to me."

She sold me on Hank Williams; I sang her Schubert's songs. Excursions were excuses to continue in her company; with them we filled the countryside. One summer, I visited her folks in Tennessee, talked law with her older brother, pitched ball with her younger. We made lots of trips to Arby's; watched lots of Little League baseball; saw county fairs with homemade foodstuffs; went to church and Sunday barbecues; visited her old schoolhouse; and, because she knew my love of politics, saw the home of some venerable congressman, "our most famous landmark," she teased, "for miles around." One afternoon she took me outside town, up remote mountain roads, where sallow eyes peered from shacks that humble people called home. "Those eyes haunt you?" she asked afterward.

"Yes. Why'd you show me?"

"I had to. I had to see how much you cared."

"Jay," she said one day after we had dated almost a year, "do you suppose that we'll get serious?"

"What do you mean? I thought we were."

"You know what I mean. Don't make me say."

I grew pale. "Anne, you can't mean marriage?"

She was silent.

"I can't believe you mean that! Isn't it enough we love each other? Why let them tame us, 'legitimize' us with their license? Do we forsake these hills for cages, the brick zoo they call the suburbs? We are free, Anne. Every minute we spend together is by choice, not because some preacher said. Why soil these moments with commitment? Why bond us to some distant day of disenchantment? Why, Anne, why?"

She was stunned. She had come prepared for a discussion but, shocked by my intemperance, thought the better of it. So the subject dropped, to no one's gain. I became nervous, knowing what was on her mind. She became frustrated, not feeling able to discuss it.

Something happened. Not that things changed suddenly. Not that they even changed directly. Not that feeling, nurtured for a year, could ever change overnight. No, it changed, if at all, by slow degrees, like the gathering grays of a long dusk. Months went by. I began to wonder whether Anne never again broached the subject of marriage because she knew of my resistance or because she herself might actually be having second thoughts. Things seemed the same. We saw no less of each other. What we did and where we went were no different than before. Was this stillness of the surface a sign of restlessness beneath? Was she less playful? Less loving? Or did I read my anxieties into her gestures, project my fears onto her face?

I began to wonder whether I had been so wise in my treatment of her on that day. Part of my wonder—I liked to think—was sensitivity to how she felt. Part of it was apprehension, only painfully articulated, that she might not always be there, to take so foolishly for granted, to lecture to the way I had that day. I began to feel an urgency, agitated by uncertainty, a wish that love would be hard oak, which one could tap every morning and have forever feel one way. I now said "I love you" because I meant it—that, for sure—but, increasingly, to receive from her some return of reassurance.

"Don't you know your real love, Jay?" she said one evening.

"Don't be silly."

"No, not me."

"Who, then?"

"Your own wanderings. I'm no more than today's material. You'll work me dry. You'll see me as I am, before your mind embroidered me. I'll stand before you plain, imperfect Anne and watch you walk away."

"Never, I love you for yourself."

"What self? The 'self' that you define for me?"

"And you wouldn't be 'defined,' as you call it, in your standardized split-foyer, with the little bridge games and car pools and shopping lists and . . ."

"So where do you propose to live? A tent? I want children. I need a mate. These days, being middle class is fatal. Too bad for us that I was born that way. I get sick. I forget. I get tired, and I complain. I'm the ordinariness that wears your love away."

"Stop! For God's sake, stop! I love you, Anne. The way you are and want to be. Marry me, Anne. Please be my wife."

Suddenly my ears rang with the echoes of adolescent rejection. Sensations stormed back, as if summoned from sleep, on the hearing of a single word—so blunt, so unkind, so flat and final. I was horrible at warding feeling from my face. Anne saw all that, and seemed shaken by her own abruptness. But she stood her ground. "So intense," she pleaded. "Always on fire." No one, she said, could withstand such ceaseless heat. Her last words were somewhere between love and pity. "It would never work for us, sweetheart," she explained, softly, in a tone that mocked the verdict. "Never in a million years."

What she left was a wreck, ears that heard but her voice, lips that felt but her kiss, eyes that saw no farther than the birthmark on her cheek. I sank back on my bed, surrounded by her absence. Those fresh first dates returned to twinge me, evenings parked in antique cars in lanes far away. I imagined the hills that had been part of our happiness. They seemed impassive now, not taking sides, nor sharing themselves with solitary travelers.

What had happened? She knew me. She treasured me.

She wished to love me to the brim, even as I jeered and poured that love away.

What was so hard, back then, about marriage? Marriage had been right for Mother and Father. Father, where were you when I needed you? How did you, forever formal at the table, turn into a prisoner of your time and place? To what senseless strike for freedom did your view of marriage fall victim, that I could see in it no ageless values of commitment, but only something not to replicate?

Would Anne patrol my mind forever, her smile life's might-have-been? Would I see her? By chance? Or by my reckoning? I rehearsed a thousand times what I should say. What if I saw her with someone in my place? What preparation would befriend me then? I *must* see her; no, never, I must not. Time heals, but over months and years; missing her was every minute. Where was she now? Enjoying what? Embracing whom? Have you ever lost someone still living? With death, at least, there is nothing to be done.

Perhaps the permissiveness of the Sixties did purge sex of paralyzing shame and guilt. Perhaps we learned the costs of soldiering on in commitments that had long since turned stone cold. But what I remember was how I learned to hold back. Always the thought that every personal relationship was provisional. Always the hope for someone better. Always the search for some new wave of sexual elation, free, disdainful, forever loath to commit. The decade brought a new credo of movement—from one place to another, from one partner to the next, forever in service of the self—that god the Sixties gave us and whom we worship still.

That god is with us in all things. Mobility and self-absorption began to phase out past togetherness. Many parents have been cut loose; children have moved too far away, and parents interfere with too much. So one watches life at Sunset Glades with its craft shops and tulip gardens and putting greens and swimming pools, and thinks how all is well. The seniors seem happy not burdening their grown children; the children seem happy unburdened by aging parents; all are happy within themselves or with their peers, just the way the self-absorbed souls of the Sixties would have wished. I can point no fingers; my dear mother lived in one of the nicest communities of all. Perhaps it's for the best, but what an extended family might have meant for her and her grandchildren I'll never really know.

The Glorious Revolution marked the ascension in 1688 of William and Mary as joint sovereigns on the English throne. But our Glorious Revolution (for that is how we regarded it back then) has not turned out so well. Soaring out-of-wedlock births. More fathers off to who knows where. More problem teens from less stable homes. Marriage more an upper-middle-class estate. The political scientist Lawrence Mead said long before the phenomenon became infinitely worse: "What matters for success is less whether your father was rich or poor than whether you knew your father at all."

Something, an awaking Rip Van Winkle would conclude, has gone very wrong. The economists talk of market volatility and growth rates and trade deficits as though they were the great barometer of social health. They are one barometer, but indicators fluctuate. Generations raised without the support and structure of a stable family will be with us for a long, long time.

I walk on fall Saturdays past fraternity row on my way to University of Virginia football games. Students are grilling burgers, playing horseshoes with beer in hand, and lounging casually on the balconies of the stately Greek houses. These are only the preliminaries, I suppose. It is scarcely high noon. A while back, *Rolling Stone* wrote an article alleging a brutal gang rape at one of the fraternity parties. The article caused a sensation, until it was discovered to be bunk. It was always hard to believe that these college students enjoying a typically fun undergraduate afternoon would ever participate in such a horrific act.

Sexual outlooks are partly generational. Yesterday's miscreants become tomorrow's scolds. Yesteryear was no bowl of roses either. Walking down a tipsy and amorous fraternity row is doubtless a whole lot more pleasant than treading the main street of one of those old Western mining towns whose chief features were the brothel and the saloon. Ah, that's it— pin the blame for sexual looseness then and now on alcohol, which, though true enough, mistakes a symptom for a cause. The whole gray zone of consent arises from such notions as "friends with benefits," from misunderstandings created by infinite casualness, from relationships whose interior ravages lie in emptiness born of transience felt not just on fraternity row but in the broken homes of those who never hoped to go to college. So we are left with a condition that has been universally diagnosed and chronically untreated. Yet by tracing its origins, we may recover the hope that virtues lost in the Sixties may one day come back in vogue.

Perhaps I lay too much blame at the doorstep of the Sixties, but I don't think so. When Elizabeth Marquardt maintains that there is no such thing for children as a "good divorce," she exaggerates, but only for emphasis—that "before the divorce rate began its inexorable rise in the late 1960s, the common wisdom had been that, where children are concerned, divorce itself is a problem." When Pamela Paul laments men who "sit in front of their computers, watching pornography and masturbating" and women "trying to please these guys by looking as much like porn stars as plastic surgery and skimpy clothing will allow," it's not hard to know this stuff got started in that preeminent pre-Internet decade.

It's not all pornography. Watching the two-piece cheerleaders, the short-skirted Wimbledon semi-finalists, the postgame interview with the female sideline commentator practically sitting in the star quarterback's lap, the alluring anchors and pundits helping me digest the worst of news—hey, it's a more pleasant world out there. What sort of guy would be ungrateful for the marketing insight of the Sixties—that feminine sway shouldn't long be out of masculine view. And it's technology, isn't it, that brought on sex as product—the Internet and television are to blame. Alas, "the fault, dear Brutus, is not in our stars, But in ourselves . . ." Count me among the countless millions not wholly chaste in thought and deed.

In the Sixties, we set sail for ourselves. Some seafaring souls know finally how elusive personal happiness can be. But it's late. It's harder to recover the capacity to love once a society cultivates a vagrant appetite for sex. It's hard also to trace hooking up and the decline of courtship to the Sixties. Causation is never simple, human nature is a constant through the centuries. I know only that loving became less in fashion in the Sixties—the times just tore away the gift.

I wonder often if the times had done that to me. Or if losing Anne was just some age-old heartache that could have happened as well a thousand years ago. Maybe it was just mixed signals and missed timing, things that bedeviled romance long before the Sixties and will continue to do so long thereafter. What it was, I'll probably never know. Still, it seems like yesterday. On the stuffed chair in my apartment in the morning lay a blue sports shirt. It lay there late at night too, when I returned. Never cleaned, never mislaid, never so slightly touched. That shirt bore the sterile air of an arrangement; nothing about it—or my apartment—held the slightest hope of a surprise. The room was too much me—everything where I had left it last. My belongings sat obediently still, like Tutankhamen's, hour after lifeless hour. Please, someone, come discover this my tomb; breathe into it life and movement and disarray. Please, someone, come release me from myself; teach me to share and give. Oh, not just someone, of course, but someone rare and crystalline to love and wed. As luck would have it, I was to find the perfect wife, but I hardly knew that then.

Two far-off decades: two kinds of loneliness. Is loneliness worse inside of marriage or out? Is loneliness the fault of one who feels it? Will I always feel it? This void—that no human company, nor God's beauty, nor eyes, fond and moon-full, will ever fill?

Jerry always told me the Sixties liberated women. Who's a man to say it isn't true? Women were chained to the kitchen and the changing table for too long. Women were undervalued in the workplace; they still are. The depth and meaning of discrimination were revealed in the Sixties, first as to blacks, but then for women too. The maturation of Sixties feminism and the modern ability to work remotely have made it possible for women to raise a family and pursue a career. I'm proud I've got a daughter who's a lawyer. The Sixties helped make this possible for her and much else too.

At what cost? The words spoken at the altar mask unspoken doubts and fears; the sexual revolution started in the Sixties leaves women lonely by the roadside as their erstwhile committed partners drive away. No one is as sure of anyone anymore. America has become too much a land of strangers. Women lose when permanence in personal matters doesn't mean what it once did.

The sad truth is that men are hurting too. The night Anne left, I could not sleep. I walked an alley, nudging with my foot an old beer can from surrounding trash, casually kicking it along out in front of me, not with my toe, but with the top of my foot, as I'd done in soccer. And the can just bumped along, wouldn't go far or straight, because of the cobblestones. Something about life, I thought, always cast us back to deal with ourselves in some sad, deserted way. It hadn't always been that way. How had lasting relationships come to seem listless and dull? How had it suddenly become so outmoded to commit? How had I turned so fiercely upon what was durable and steadfast? But my eyes welled up, and I thought of her, ran up, crazy kicked the can until it banged and caromed through the dark. Maybe we're all now in back-alley motion. Maybe we'll never know how or when to stop.

III. The Demise of Law

LONG AFTER THE 1960S, I had the good fortune to become a federal judge. Litigation is never in short supply, and in most cases the law seems to work pretty well. But America's legal culture is also terribly divided—over abortion, affirmative action, capital punishment, church-state relations, executive authority, war powers, and many other things.

To a great extent, these divisions in the law reflect nothing more than divisions within our country at large. It has always been so. But the current divide has an ominous edge. Liberals and conservatives want their view of religious practice or abortion or gay rights to be the law, whatever the cost. And if they can nail down their view of things in our Constitution, so much the better.

Ideology über alles was the mantra of the Sixties, but it has done the law incalculable harm. The idea that the end justifies the means is the very opposite of what the law was meant to be. Yet in the 1960s, the end became everything, and law became, like politics or demonstrations or even riots, just another means of getting to wherever it is one wants to

go. When that happens, law lacks its own integrity. There is
no rule of law left, only the propensities and impulses of men.

The goal of racial justice was a noble one, and ending the
Vietnam War seemed almost as urgent by the close of the
decade. Law had brought the civil rights struggle a long way,
but increasingly, as the Sixties progressed, violence began to
supplant it. So we reaped the whirlwind of chaotic campuses,
ravaged cities, and assassinated leaders, all because people felt
their own view of what was right supplanted their obligation
to respect the general view reflected in the law.

It would be a mistake to think rebelliousness began in
the 1960s. Rampant lawlessness did not begin in the 1960s
either—the night riders of the Ku Klux Klan and the speak-
easies of Al Capone's Chicago attest to that. We Americans
are by nature a rambunctious people—what else but a rebellion gave us birth? George Washington had to call out troops
to subdue the Whiskey Rebellion in 1794. Lincoln had to
still by force the Rebel Yell. There has been no end of labor
unrest and forcible repression. And let's not forget the anar-
chists: the Chicago Haymarket Riot of 1886 and the slaying
of President McKinley in 1901 led to a law prohibiting them
from coming to America. One can make the case that a certain contrarian spirit is the soulmate of liberty or, conversely,
that the violence that often accompanies obstreperous acts is
liberty's greatest threat. How else to explain the ambivalence
that surrounds the glorious abolitionist / demonic killer John
Brown to this very day?

Given all this, it is not fair to single out one decade as the
sole cause of every renewed period of American unrest. So
why then do I point to the Sixties as lawlessness writ large?
Because it was, most especially in its later years. Past lawlessness sometimes faded with the particular grievance that gave

rise to it. But the Sixties seemed more to impart to lawlessness a modus operandi that has been and will be adapted to many different causes over many years to come. Then, too, the bootleggers and moonshiners who operated during Prohibition were more in the nature of legal evaders, as marijuana users are now. The rioters, assassins, and more radical campus protesters of the Sixties sought not to evade the law but to annihilate it, as did the Southern demagogues who spewed contempt for law at schoolhouse doors. There is a difference between evasion and annihilation. Both are bad, but only one presents a mortal threat.

To the good folks who protest I overstate the influence of the 1960s, let me caution gently against the malady of Sixties Denial, which rejects considering the decade as a large contributing cause of America's present ills. Nowhere has this been truer than with the law.

Will the disrespect for law sown during the 1960s break into the open contempt likewise sanctioned during that decade? People assure me that the 1960s will never be repeated. But look around. The example of the Sixties still remains. Social volcanoes go quiet for a time, only to erupt when crisis conditions come again. We are a changed country because of the Sixties, more prone to molten protest and destruction than before. There will be a next time and a next, and I worry that law may not stand in its way. Much of its stature was shaken long ago.

"The Law." The Dean spoke with a hush, as if in the presence of a deity. "I have," he confided, "an unabashed, undiluted love of The Law."

In September 1967 we arrived at the University of Virginia Law School. The Dean, along in years, had become a

legend. He was one of those who had communed with The
Law; no one doubted that. The Law had cloaked its ser-
vant in all its pomp and majesty, and now he spoke atop the
mountain of authority.

The Law had imposed its marvelous order on the chaos
of human affairs, he declared. Criminal law secured man's
person. Property law secured his possessions. Contract law
secured his expectations. Tort law secured him from un-
expected misfortune. Family law secured his hearth. Estate
law secured his inheritance. Tax law secured the blessings
of government. The secure man, the Dean intoned, was less
tempted to revert to the savage state.

Even that, remarkably, failed to do justice to the power of
The Law. "Laws are the great riverbanks between which society flows," the Dean continued. Progress and achievement
owed its being to the influence of The Law. "Architects of
a stable society," he concluded, "that's what lawyers are and
will ever be."

It didn't dawn on us at first that we were about to study
law in one of the most lawless decades ever. You don't often
think of the big picture when you're struggling to survive. If
the Sixties posed one giant question to authority, it was still
not the place of fledgling law students to question the Dean's
view. Besides, I couldn't figure law school out. Classes ran on
the currency of Socratic method: a question was worth more
than an answer, and one obscure answer more than a dozen
clear ones. In grateful appreciation of this approach, students
labeled one class "mystery hour," and another twelve o'clock
session "darkness at noon."

"What is it, young man, A or B?" the professor asked.

"A," I said confidently.

"No!"

"Well then, B."

"No!"

I felt my classmates smiling. Not A, not B. Where, for heaven's sake, was C? The answer must be somewhere, and I wanted to take a sledgehammer and slam down hard on its head.

"Well . . . ," said the professor. Nothing was so lethal in this profession as silence.

We proceeded through classes much as our predecessors had. The venerable canons of the common law were remote from the passions roiling the world outside. In Property class, we learned of bailments and bona fide purchasers, in Contracts of offer, acceptance, and consideration—rote lessons of The Law since the days of Blackstone. Lawyers delighted in categories; we studied *res judicata* and learned what *alternate legal contingent remainders in fee simple* were and *express promissory dependent conditions precedent* (the latter being the law's answer to the structure of a protein molecule).

As in college, our formal education seemed detached from contemporary conflict. Oh sure, we law students studied conflict aplenty, but it was mostly of the private, trivial sort. The word "conflict" in college meant momentous arguments over civil rights and Vietnam. The endless personal quarrels we read about in law school seemed almost demeaning to the student minds the Sixties nurtured. Why, law school went so far as to reduce people and principles alike to algebraic symbols (O sues A for Blackacre). Someone was always accusing someone else of breaching his contract, taking his property, trampling his rights. In a Domestic Relations course, we learned how husband and wife could not live together; in Torts, how people couldn't move without injuring one another; in Trusts, how fiduciaries breached du-

ties toward others; in Contracts, how apparent meetings of
minds erupted in misunderstandings.

All these endless private squabbles seemed petty and selfish and ever so bourgeois. The whole point of the Sixties was
to move beyond such things. Had law no vision of this better
day? Had law nothing to do with human harmonies? Cases
exposed mainly prey and predator, the whole lush habitat of
the human jungle. Did hospitals immunize doctors to death?
Then courtrooms hardened lawyers to the imaginative ways
people gouge each other while alive.

I might have succumbed to that view of things, but the
Dean would not hear of it. It was in the resolution of conflict that The Law was most ennobling. The human beast, he
said, would either take up his club or seek satisfaction in the
courtroom. "Which, my dear fellow, would you choose?"
The Law, he told me, had verbalized aggression. By reducing
conflict to mere words, The Law had tamed and civilized it.
It was but a short step from words to reason and then from
reason to understanding. The grand thing about the adversary
system, he reminded, "was having to listen to your adversary's case."

The Dean and the lowliest first-year law student were
agreed on one thing. There was to be law school and nothing else. Devotion was the Dean's thing—you knew just by
looking at him that he had given wholly of himself. So, too,
my previous life was to be beside the point. *The Law Covets
Your Every Waking Moment*, read the cover to a magazine. At
Yale, I had outgrown homework, but now again I was a
schoolboy, demeaned by daily preparations. Law school contracted thought and, like some angry accordionist, squeezed
out all the air. Everything had to be reunderstood. There was
layman's time, and then there was legal time, where "the day

of the act, event, or default from which the designated period of time begins to run shall not be included." It was all very precise. I thought in square corners and I walked in straight lines. In self-defense, I turned into a syllogism.

But it wasn't only devotion to the law that sealed so many law students off from the Sixties. Social consciousness was less important than the $15,000 salary offered to first-year associates by Cravath, Swaine and Moore. That salary was the talk of the school. It conveyed the stirring message of how important we were. It also carried the weight of human bondage. Of the myopia of our labor there would be no doubt. New York paid the highest salaries and New York did the best S-1 forms. We were to be schooled in the details of draftsmanship. At that price, who could protest?

The Sixties insisted we not snuff out our better selves: the recruiters for these corporate firms seemed a suffocating insult to all that we believed. For a time, I was tempted to quit law school and go to graduate school in history. Law would squinch our souls, but history, with its Napoleons and Churchills, its Middle Ages and Age of Pericles, must abound in scope and vision. The great historians created character, atmosphere, narrative tension; they had the novelist's gifts anchored by truth. The historian's joy was to soar back before his birthdate, to sit in Thomas Jefferson's parlor, to endure Lincoln's great siege. Exploration . . . that was freedom, while law school was a ball and chain.

The Dean's eyes twinkled just when it seemed the moment could not, for the life of it, become more earnest. He was a disconcerting man, an *éminence grise* who could quote Yogi Berra. His demeanor left no doubts. One looked at him and supposed law school the only place to be, at least for someone with a nickel's worth of sense. Why go to graduate school? The Law, he reminded, was the highest form of history.

The Law matured. The Law adapted. The Law, declared the Dean, had the marvelous invention known as precedent, which ensured that history was constantly revised even as it was continually consulted. Precedent stood as the great guardian against radical change; The Law had mastered the art of evolution. Old cases, said the Dean, *Kingston v. Preston, Brown v. Kendall, Swift v. Tyson, Dred Scott, Plessy v. Ferguson*, ruled as long, and as regrettably, as any Napoleon. Just when The Law seemed buried by its past, the seeds of peaceful regeneration sprang up within the system of precedent. Precedent, he said, embodied George Bernard Shaw's advice to his generation: "We must not stay as we are, doing always what was done last time, or we shall stick in the mud. Yet neither must we undertake a new world as catastrophic Utopians, and wreck our civilization in our hurry to mend it."

The Dean's eyes took on their distant look. While he was living a vision, I was lucky to get my daily assignments done. The Law might indeed be great, but what did one little law student matter? My grasp of things kept slipping—causation, jurisdiction, reliance, estoppel all unconnected in my head. As a child, when I said ridiculous things, my parents used to tell me of the boy who, with every silly utterance, kept shrinking in size until one day he got lost for good under the sofa. The Law made a first-year law student feel just that small.

So, if not history, then politics. That, not law, might be my calling. How could law compete with the fanfare of a convention, the rituals of the Senate, the pace and tempo of a tough campaign? What mere lawyer debated war and peace or the spending of unfathomable sums? Law cloistered people in the small circle of their clients; politics launched them large into the world.

Besides, studying law was sedentary. Politics was motion. Motion was getting somewhere. Sitting down was going no-where—or so it felt. I looked at campaign itineraries—nine stops a day. In law school all you did was move from class to class.

Two summers before law school, I had chauffeured Wil-lis Robertson, a United States Senator from Virginia, in a hotly contested primary election. Robertson was real old-time; he salted his rhetoric with quotations from Jonathan Edwards, Shakespeare, and the Bible; he warned of Ahab and his vineyard, spoke of armageddons and of Gabriel's horn. On the stump he could be fearsome, peering down on audi-ences from thick, bushy brows. All the July days he stumped, at catfish fries and barbecues. He spoke hard, pumping his fists, and shook hands until even his strong grip was sore. What had law to compare to his quest, to the delicious ex-haustion of one last voter won?

In 1970, in the middle of law school, I left to run for Con-gress. I won the Republican nomination and faced a conser-vative incumbent Democrat, David Satterfield, in the general election. The campaign was something of a lark. I had little chance of winning, but blasting an opponent's record sure beat being in law school. My strategy was to sweep the black and labor voters who were disenchanted with Satterfield and capture enough of the increasingly Republican suburbs for a victory. One trouble I had was that I was supposed to deliver to the Lee-Davis Country Club on Saturday and to black church groups on Sunday a consistent and equally inspiring message.

There was yet another problem. I looked younger than my twenty-five years. The campaign managers and consultants were afraid to use my picture. So they resorted to radio ads with deep, husky voice-overs, and to etchings, not photographs. When a picture absolutely had to be used, I was surrounded by senior citizens. My opponent had a slogan to capitalize on that: "Send Satterfield back to Congress and Wilkinson back to school." The voters generously took up that suggestion.

Somehow I was not disheartened by this defeat, but so exhilarated by the prospect of holding public office that I prepared to run the next year for the state legislature. As a matter of courtesy, I stopped in to inform the Dean that I was about to abandon my legal education. I was prepared for him to try to talk me out of it, and I was even more determined not to let him do so.

Cheer up, he said. If it was glamour that I wanted, The Law had a glamour all its own. Most people were well diverted from remaking the world to make a living. And The Law, he was wont to say, was not only a good way to make a living but a grand way to make a life. He would never, it seemed, place his dignity at the sufferance of politics. Politics made men supplicants; The Law alone made them statesmen. Politics brewed passions; The Law treasured reason.

The glory of the judicial process, he believed, was that it did not rush to judgment. And so, as seemed fitting, the Dean was made a judge. It was said, shortly after his appointment to the International Court of Justice, or World Court, that a neighbor met him at the gate of his Rugby Road home and inquired, "How am I supposed to address you now?" And the Dean replied, inscrutably, "Holiness, I suppose, will do."

There comes a time, I think, when one simply stops resisting. My campaign had been a bust, and everyone but me knew it. The Dean put it gently—that he wasn't cut out for politics either. He offered me not a consolation prize but what was dearer to him than life: The Law. The Law was like a foreign language; one day you stop fighting it and start thinking it. Before kissing my date, I found myself pondering the full import of offensive battery and dignitary tort. The day a car almost hit me, I went home and wrote a holographic will. I was getting fancy with my tax returns. I watched myself on the verge of contract with the auto mechanic and the soda jerk. We were being trained "to think like lawyers"—that mystic phrase, which meant, I suppose, investing life's more inconsequential moments with legal significance.

"I see you're telling me to drive 55 mph. Why not 65? I'm in a bit of a hurry."

"Oh, come," says the speed limit. "You can answer that. Because there's too much carnage at 65."

"If you're worried about that, why don't you make me drive 50. If you said 50, you'd save more lives."

"Maybe, but people wouldn't go as fast as they want to. And if I said 50, they wouldn't respect me anyway."

"Not respect you? You're the law!"

"That's not enough these days. And besides, being a law doesn't give me the right to be unreasonable."

"The people that made you thought you were reasonable."

"It's what the people who obey think that counts these days. And I'm sensitive about stepping on their rights."

"Stepping on their rights? How do you do that?"

"By not letting them drive as fast as they want to."

"Wait a minute. When did they get that right?"

"Just lately, it seems. If they want to drive faster than 55, perhaps they should be able to."

"Cut that out. If you're a law, then act like one. I don't

want speed limits like you pussyfooting around the highways.
I got my rights too, you know. Like not being in a crash. If
I'm to heed you, make damn sure that green Chevy does also."

"Well, I still I think I should be changed. Instead of saying 'Maximum Safe Speed 55 mph,' I'd like to say 'Please
drive 55 mph.' Then I wouldn't hurt so many feelings."

"Hurt feelings! A good law can't be friends with everybody. Someone's going to hate you."

"Yeah, they used to. Hated or loved, but never ignored."

"Oh, quit feeling sorry for yourself."

"Well, I've a right to. I'm not doing the job. All us laws
feel in the dumps these days. Me, I haven't kept the highways
safe. People die under my eyes. And then I get up the gump-
tion to yell, 'Drive 55, for your own sake,' but they ignore
me, especially you young people. And if I haven't kept people safe, I haven't gotten them where they want to go, either.
They're angry at me now for tie-ups. What's a law to do?"

Law indeed was on the run. We read where some 250
black students from Florida A&M marched to protest the arrest of their schoolmates and segregation in the county jail.
Asked by the sheriff to leave the premises, many refused, singing freedom songs and clapping, blocking the jail's entrance
and driveway, until they were arrested too. As we pondered
the most venerable of laws, that of trespass, put at the disposal
of the most corrupt of practices, that of segregation, it seemed
that my friend the speed limit had been right: law was sorely
beset.

What was the spirit of the Sixties, the lawmaker's authority or the lawbreaker's arrest? What mattered, the closing
statements in the courtroom or the provocation in the street?
Fire became the new mode of expression: flags in flame,
to protest the war; draft cards burned on courthouse steps.

Speakers were shouted down, offices overrun, police pelted, judges insulted—was it because law had cast its lot with Lyndon Baines Johnson, become high executioner of the war, henchman for the draft and Army—not a beacon of freedom, but authority's brute boot?

I remember one summer driving through the countryside of eastern North Carolina. It was the state's "black belt," where the only folks not farming seemed to work in tractor dealerships on the edge of town. Suddenly, right in the middle of a tobacco field, standing guard like a scarecrow, was an "Impeach Earl Warren" sign. It had been bleached by the sun, but it was clear the farmer was not shrinking from it, and I supposed the sign was repainted with each planting. Tobacco farming was hard work, and it struck me that this was the one message the farmer wanted in the field, hour after hour, to console him: Impeach Earl Warren. I wanted to laugh, but I kept asking: Why did this ugly sign mean so much? Because, of course, the farmer believed himself God-fearing, segregationist, and a patriot, and there was Earl Warren, tearing down his world.

No wonder my speed limit felt so helpless. All laws did. What mere law could unite the anti-war activist and the anti-Warren farmer? Somehow the same law was supposed to govern both, yet the activist identified courts with repression, the farmer with a revolution. So both had taken to their posters, and law got cursed from all sides.

With law, as in so many areas, the climate of the Sixties seemed to push for an all-or-nothing choice: total allegiance or total contempt. I wondered what the Dean would say about all this. He was, I knew, the reason I remained in school at a time when I was tempted by a thousand other things. Yet his influence was not that of a friend, or even a counselor, for

I mostly saw him walking corridors, and mainly heard him from a platform. At the law school, he was less talked to than talked about; he instructed by example from afar. William Osler said once that "no bubble is so iridescent or floats longer than that blown by the successful teacher," when the pupil imitates the mentor, not so much in action or in manner, but in the intimacy of thought. So I found myself thinking that The Law would also show the middle way. The Court under Earl Warren opened the arteries of change, broadened the franchise, equalized access to schools and facilities, gave the common man the First Amendment, and donated to a society in turmoil its lasting gift of peaceful change.

Whether the Dean would have put it that way I doubted, but the sentiment was surely his. He would make of The Law a rock to cling to, more than that, a veritable mountain of stability and justice thrusting high above the turmoil of the Sixties, towering over the encircling din.

Our great hope was that Vietnam would be settled not by arms but by diplomacy. It was as far as I could see. The Dean hoped all that and more. Even diplomacy, he told us once, was "episodic." Diplomatic solutions were inherently "ad hoc," abating momentary tensions without the predictability needed for an ordered world. The world might lessen tensions only by absorbing them within a legal system. The practical difficulties to international law were prodigious, and he recounted all of them. "But . . . ," he said, "world peace might one day be possible, with a mighty contribution from The Law."

Nothing is so poignant as a man who keeps faith as his world crashes around him. The Dean's world crashed in the 1960s, and his beloved law became a bloodied anachronism. The Law might regulate the formation of contracts, but it

had nothing to say to the smoldering cities. To watch the
rioters in Watts was to sense the law's impotence. The Law
had not only failed to check black rage; the "motherfucking"
cops ignited it. Those rocks and bottles weren't just heaved
at passing motorists; they were aimed straight at The Law.
Didn't the Dean know that the Watts riots broke out four
days after the Voting Rights Act took effect? Law had become irrelevant to life on the street, and the tales that had
served the Dean in such good stead for so many student generations—legendary fables of peppercorns and the like—now
seemed faded in the face of the urban fires.

What the Dean saw as an object of reverence became
an agent of oppression. Bull Connor placed The Law at the
service of brutality; George Wallace used The Law of his
state to defy the dictates of a national constitution. Law itself thus sank in esteem. Arrest became a badge of honor—
the hallowed moments of the decade were those spent by
King in a Birmingham jail. Soon enough, all restraint would
be removed. "It is a miracle," warned Malcolm X, "that
twenty-two million black people have not risen up against
their oppressors—in which they would have been justified
by all moral criteria . . ." Thus exonerated, the mobs took to
the streets exhilarated. Slogans—Black Power, Burn, Baby,
Burn—served as the fuse. The Dean's world was gone with
the flames and the wind.

Even on the Dean's own turf, the campus, The Law
came into disrepute. Law was, after all, a system of rules, but
the belief of the Sixties was that rules existed to be broken.
As events in Birmingham energized the civil rights movement, events in Vietnam energized the campus. Sit-ins at
soda fountains inspired sit-ins at administration buildings.
The Law seemed on the outs; disobedience seemed in.

As the war's toll mounted, so did campus violence. "Professors learned to live with bomb threats," wrote Garry Wills. "A vestige of student politeness made one demonstrator ask a friend of mine to leave his office in an administration building so they could set it on fire." If the cities had been moved by the hopelessness of poverty, the students were tormented by the aimlessness of affluence. So a counterculture of bearded rebels and beaded drifters soon emerged. The Weathermen wanted to stone The Law; the Yippies simply to urinate upon it. Yippies demanded the abolition of money, and legislation permitting people to "fuck all the time, anytime, whomever they want. . . ." What there was left of The Law became reserved for ridicule.

The irony was that the 1960s witnessed real triumphs of law, most notably the Civil Rights Act of 1964, the Voting Rights Act of 1965, and the *Miranda* and reapportionment decisions of the Warren Court itself. Side by side with all their lawlessness, the Sixties showcased law's potential for bringing peaceful change. The tragedy was that all the progressive legislation and enlightened Court decisions seemed to make no difference. The riots and assassinations and disdain for rights of others only escalated on both the right and the left. And those who led change early in the decade were themselves overwhelmed by lawlessness by the end.

Events seemed to engulf even Earl Warren. "On the morning of March 31, 1966," he wrote, "David Paul O'Brien and three companions burned their Selective Service registration certificates on the steps of the South Boston Courthouse. A sizable crowd, including several agents of the Federal Bureau of Investigation, witnessed the event. Immediately after the burning, members of the crowd began attacking O'Brien and his companions. . . . O'Brien stated to FBI agents that he had burned his registration certificate because of his beliefs, knowing that he was violating federal law." That the Supreme Court eventually upheld the convictions amounted to no more than a judicial finger in the dike. What was protest to some was treason to others, and passions were leaving The Law in the dust.

None of this, of course, was helping me to prepare for final exams. Law school exams were jumbo trembles, the entire year's grade riding on a three-hour test in June. There must be a medical term for examination nightmares:

> *With clock tick, ticking on the wall,*
> *Cannot recall, cannot recall.*

The only way to prepare was to pretend you did not live. Daily indulgences such as shaving and the sports section were shoved aside. The course outline accompanied me to the bathroom. I couldn't decide whether I wanted the exams to come or not. They were rumored to be not exercises in regurgitation but inductions into the rigors of analysis. No, I definitely did *not* want them to come. Anticipation was a horror exceeded only by the event.

Well, of course, they came. All except Contracts. It was last, and the hardest to make myself study for. So I got my study food, a huge box of Sugar Corn Pops, snatched some FM station, and settled down for the night. I was reviewing the area of minors' contracts—whether one should hold 16-year-olds to bad bargains where the adult party had negotiated in good faith—and I was getting ever so slightly interested when suddenly the radio turned grave.

There it was again. The lethal footage run and rerun (I had now turned on the television), the pained horror of bystanders, the practiced cadence of the media, the instant

celebrity of the psychopath, the instant manufacture of re-
membrances, the reshuffle of the political deck (the decent
interval for TV deaths was twenty minutes)—assassinations
had usurped conventions as the political rituals of our times.

I rushed to Sherry's apartment. Sherry and I had lately
been at odds. But tonight there was a truce; I offered her
my Sugar Pops. I could not believe what my TV was saying.
Could I listen to hers? Her set was different, and maybe mine
had lied.

I had always had excuses to dismiss Robert Kennedy.
Cocksure and insecure. To prove himself, he flattened everyone he knew. Not like Jack. Robert's vision was something
he smacked into. When he visited the ghetto and the Delta,
I was wary. When he traveled to the reservations, I was cool.
When he called on migratory labor, I was indifferent. When
he spoke of the coal mines, I had been unmoved. Then I
faced the draft and Robert Kennedy opposed The War, and
I said, here at last was a man who grew.

Even now, on the night of his death, still I wondered
what I mourned. Was it for the man and his family? For the
country and its loss? For the dispossessed without a champion? Or for something far more selfish—had I loved only
his last cause?

It was a long night, one where hope broke faith, where
death stalked dreams anew. A night beyond comfort, where
Sherry was a perfect host, because she felt free to speak aloud
dark moods. There was a scene from the Nebraska primary
where a breeze blew Kennedy's speech into the crowd, and
he had yelped, "Give me that back. That's my farm program." On and on in self-deprecating humor, the Robert
Kennedy nobody knew. But Sherry said now that she knew
why he was shot, because these were the days when death
stalked laughter too.

It is supposed to be a relief, amid death, to have things that one must do. So I stared at the Contracts book before me. Its pages turned slowly in the best of times. Now they froze, and I thought I had lost the ability to read, or, rather, to read anything so trifling as a contract again. All it implied—its promised land of stability and predictability—was unworthy of belief that evening, or any evening when a bullet decided to reroute history anew.

I got no sleep that night. At first, I thought, surely the school would postpone this thing. But the examination took no cognizance of grogginess. It featured the most gruesome business problem, one probing the penumbras of the Uniform Commercial Code. Somehow I managed to hand something in. It was horrible, but maybe the papers would be uniformly horrible, and we'd all stagger through. It was, I thought, fitting that my last exam that year was Contracts; the thing that would not cease for death was commerce; funerals were fertile ground for bargains too.

I left law school in low spirits, as if, suddenly, a hoax had been revealed. The Law could not bring back Robert Kennedy. It could avenge, but it could not restore or heal. It could assess damages, it could impose sentences; like any sovereign, it could whip and flail. The Law was left to salvage what it could for refugees from mishap, but it had no balm for the stricken, no solace; it stood impotent in the end, the rule of Law in its full majestic futility, the emperor with no clothes.

I had seen the Dean that day walking down the law school steps as he always did. Behind him the columns and the two great urns. Above him the motto: THAT THOSE ALONE MAY BE SERVANTS OF THE LAW WHO LABOR WITH LEARNING, COURAGE AND DEVOTION TO PRESERVE LIBERTY AND PROMOTE JUSTICE. The death of last evening would have saddened him, but not shaken him. That was the difference. I watched him now from a widening distance. What would it take to make him understand? The faith he lived had become a thing unto itself, impervious even to the evidence his profession craved.

Like the Dean, Robert Kennedy believed in the system. On race, he believed in the capacity of The Law, that stateways could change folkways. As Attorney General, he was The Law against those who drew their lines of defiance in the dust. On Vietnam, he represented peace through peaceful change, through an election. He said of the radical students what he said of the reactionary segregationists: "If we let this hatred and emotion control our lives, we're lost." As much as any man, Robert Kennedy represented the shining promise of The Law—and couldn't the Dean see that with his death something of The Law died too?

In the end, chaos seemed to consume everyone and everything. Not even assassination could bring to the Sixties a suitable period of peace and mourning. The Chicago police and National Guardsmen and rampaging demonstrators at the Democratic Convention in 1968 gave vent to violent hatreds, but not a thought to the rule of law or vision of America to which Robert Kennedy gave his life.

One tiny thing I could do, I thought, was await the issuance of a Robert F. Kennedy postage stamp. As a stamp collector, I used to send my letters with commemoratives. It's a small, but sincere, way to express grief or admiration. But it's a tricky business; if the recipient doesn't like the event or person being commemorated, you can get blowback even from old friends. When the Postal Service recently issued American flag stamps marked LIBERTY, JUSTICE, FREEDOM, or EQUALITY, I figured these were stamps so generic and dull that no one could raise an objection. Not much for a philatelist

perhaps, but perfect for me as a judge, because they expressed
the great substantive goals of law. But law is just as much a
commitment to process as it is to ends and aspirations—to
holding hearings and harvesting evidence. And our Constitution is, above all, a tribute to process on a grand scale—a
sacred commitment that we as a society will settle differences
a certain way. Through elections and legislation and litigation
the process would bring respect for adverse outcomes and
(hopefully) for those who disagree. The problem is that process requires patience and trust, two qualities that since the
explosions of the 1960s and the disillusionment of Watergate
have been in short supply.

In the courtroom these days, all seems well. Oyez, Oyez
(Hear ye, hear ye), all stand as the judges arrive, and counsel,
law clerks, courtroom deputies, and the public take their ac-
customed seats. The raised bench, the black robes, the dark
suits, the rarefied crackle of questions, the ritual intonations
of "May it please the court," all this would not lead one to
suspect that beyond the solemnity within the walls lies a fractured society into which even the most heated courtroom
arguments afford no more than a small glimpse.

I know as a judge that law draws its life from assent, not
coercion; from citizens who carry an allegiance to the legal
order in their hearts. And as much as I love the law, I would
love it even more if every citizen who left my courtroom
would have just a tiny bit more faith in those four beautiful words on the postage stamps. But faith in government,
business, academia, the church, and institutions of all sorts
weakens in a rancorous and cynical social order, and how
do I communicate to those before me in the courtroom that
they should nonetheless have faith in law? How, when jury
verdicts in Florida and grand jury decisions in New York

and police brutalities in Baltimore, Charleston, and Chicago ignite unrest across the country, do I amid all the understandable frustration and mistrust let folks in my small courtroom know that law remains the tie that binds, the best hope we still have. Perhaps the Dean could do that, maybe, but I fear most mornings it's beyond my power to make four simple words on postage stamps truly come alive.

Do I blame the 1960s? Yes, in part, I do. Their lawlessness begot lawlessness, infecting even law enforcement itself. So we watched as Richard Nixon, who campaigned on "law and order," became the very embodiment of lawlessness. So we saw the infamous Cincinnati branch of the Internal Revenue Service turn even the law of taxation to political ends. So we observed in 2014 contempt for law from those entrusted with law, as NYPD officers, in defiance of their regulations, administered death by strangulation to Eric Garner, an unarmed African American, for selling a few loose unlicensed cigarettes. So we witnessed protesters blocking streets and bridges, disrupting commuters with "die-ins" on the floor of Grand Central Station, and shoppers with "march-ins" at Macy's and the Apple Store. So we recoiled at the retaliatory killings of two police officers in Brooklyn. "The system is guilty. Burn it down," read one sign in Times Square. So we wonder why those not part of any "system" must watch their livelihoods burn down before their eyes.

In Chicago, March 2016, a mob gathered to force the cancellation of a presidential candidate's political rally. And the candidate egged on supporters who would rough up and punch out protesters who dared to disagree with him. Free speech and assembly were assaulted on all sides. The disruptionist ethos of the Sixties lives on; somewhere its tacticians must be smiling. It is human to seek at least something meaningful in everything, but nihilism, as its name implies, scorns even the attempt of civilized order to explain it. A free society welcomes a certain ebullience in protest and tolerates a certain inconvenience, but not the smashed windows and wrecked storefronts that accompanied the Garner protests in that cradle of Sixties activism, Berkeley, California.

It is said that only a "tiny minority" of students caused campus disruptions in the 1960s and that only a tiny minority of New Orleans residents shot at the rescue helicopters in the aftermath of Hurricane Katrina, and that only a tiny minority of Occupy Wall Street members were actually arrested, and that only a tiny minority of a great religious faith would ever visit devastation upon the Boston Marathon, as though destructive weaponry and media amplification had not empowered tiny minorities far beyond their numbers. While a "tiny minority" may draw attention to not-so-tiny injustices, and while small groups may in some instances serve as the conscience of the larger community, it becomes difficult to hear a message of conscience from messengers who trample all rights but their own. How was it that the decade of the Sixties bequeathed to us a "new normal" of vandalism and disruption, along with the smoldering Sixties question: Will it ever end?

From time to time, we all feel misunderstood. Even majorities can be misread (white Southerners are not all bigots) and everyone feels compelled to blurt at some point, "Hold it. You don't know me!" Only a utopian believes we can in some way switch lives, so that a white policeman could live for a day as a black teenager from a public housing project or that same teenager could spend a day as a policeman on a dangerous beat. Courtrooms, though, do bring awareness that breakfast, lunch, and dinner are not, for all Americans, the same. To steep oneself in scenes from other lives might be a start, but law too is a connective tissue, and to reject it for violence against arrestees or policemen—or whomever—brings hope for human understanding to a halt. "You don't know me, judge"—that is true, I don't, not well enough, for my own earliest recollection of a policeman is of someone who lifted me high on his beautiful brown horse to give me a ride. But will we ever understand the only partial truth of earliest memory when violence visited on our fellow countrymen, black and white, comes continually to cloud and complicate the task?

It must have been my fond childhood memories of police, repeated many times since in amicable conversation and interaction, that made it difficult to comprehend what happened in the 1960s. When I visited New York University a decade back to give a talk, I decided to walk to nearby Stonewall Inn, where a police raid on the patrons of a tavern in 1969 became a landmark event in the history of gay rights. It was broad daylight, and the tavern itself had a rather dark and unprepossessing look. Across the street was a tiny park and two small statues of same-sex couples. Surprised by such inconspicuous reminders of such a major historical event, I supposed that one day there would come national recognition, as is now rightly proposed, to fully commemorate Stonewall's monumentality. But then I thought that the understated scene also served to remind one of the daily comings and goings of that community and the gratuitousness of police cruelty inflicted upon it. Birmingham, Chicago, Stonewall, Kent State—events that at the time seemed spaced apart—become compressed and even combustible in memory. To believe that the police function is central to civilized order is not to deny that law was damaged in the 1960s by both those obliged to obey and those sworn to uphold it. We have been living with both sad legacies ever since.

The 1960s had started so differently. The nonviolent civil disobedience of the early civil rights movement had been more than benign—it was uplifting. But early in the decade many made the grave miscalculation that lawbreaking could be limited to good causes. They seemed not to recognize, until too late, what a mindless monster they had sired. Beyond the mayhem lay a sort of stalking madness, a prowling indulgence in the commission of crimes without compunction. In loosening the constraints of law, we brought upon ourselves a final, haunting question: were those who slew the true heroes of the Sixties persons whom, in some deranged way, the decade's lawless spirit had launched forth?

More and more, I have come to suspect the answer might be yes. Not that we know why the leaders of that age were killed. But by the end of the Sixties, poisoned minds took upon themselves the license that purer protests had earlier taken with the law. After the Sixties, there would be no end to the slaughter that in the lawbreaker's mind seemed just. The jihadists of 9/11 and its long aftermath of terror have this at least in common with the worst moments of the decade: a belief that contempt for the civilizing force of law could only hasten the dawn of one's own right and perfect day.

It is possible to see law, like Caesar's Gaul, as divided into three parts: those who make law, those who enforce and interpret it, and those who obey it. And the more bridges you can build among those three parts, the more law approaches the high end of Justice. The problem is that even best friends can see Justice in different but quite defensible ways. Law mediates those differences—at least in an imperfect world composed of imperfect beings, we have found no

better way. Law recognizes that no political creed has any
monopoly on truth or wisdom, as much as the pious of every
persuasion would have us think otherwise. Forsaking law for
the consuming fires of zealotry leaves this poor world prey
to the ever more dangerous and annihilative depredations
that modern capacities make possible. The stakes are just that
large. And I worry, despite myself and not just in the wee
hours, that I will discover that my fear is no false alarm.

Tragedy is never just impersonal. In the end, the Sixties
shattered the Dean's grand vision of The Law. They reduced
to rubble the dreams of a noble man. The Dean alone seemed
not to recognize it. His dress was as dignified, his eyes as
steady, his hair as much in place, his gait as regular as ever. He
would look no different on this, the last day of class. What
was he thinking? He was such a puzzle. My understanding of
him would have to wait for another day. Why would someone place hope in reason that was no match for madness, in
order that was at the mercy of chaos, in a temple whose light
shone only for priests in the darkness of the tomb?

IV. The Loss of Home

THE LEGAL EDICTS of segregation may have seemed the same. But the ways in which segregation dehumanized were very different. Segregation could take crude and mean forms. But in the privileged precincts of the South of my boyhood, it may have been its vast silences that hurt the most. Things were seldom examined, never discussed. Because of that, the practice of segregation could seem almost preordained, an everlasting order whose changeless rhythms left those it harmed almost without hope. Only those silences could have helped the system last as long as it did. Where it was openly defended, the defenders were routed and took flight. Many whites whom segregation ostensibly "benefited" came in time to see it as a burden too. We were born into a world whose other halves and full realities we were scarcely allowed to glimpse.

Segregation was the shameful part of my childhood, but it was thankfully not all of it. There was much given to me in my boyhood, but the gifts were not all monetary. The chief gift was a string of simple words—duty, honor, country, character, courage, trust, and truth. Those words became our rocks. My world was short on ambiguity and qualification, but there was no shortage of absolutes. So one grew up anchored, fortified by constancy. And when life's temptations and difficulties came at us, as they inevitably did, there were always those words to fall back on; even when we strayed or rebelled, we knew very clearly what we were straying from and rebelling against.

We think we know what "home" means when we may not. Long after its last brick is laid in place, a home may yet build life's foundations, and I shall always be grateful that mine did. But home shelters one not only from the wind and rain but also from life's lessons, some of which I was late to learn. When I say I lost my home in the 1960s, it was in the best and worst sense. My eyes opened, and I saw at long last many things, among them my own blindness.

"Wash up!" they hollered.

"Just a minute. Man's on third and gotta hit him home."

"Supper's ready and now."

I rushed, swung at a bad pitch, and yelled in at them for making me miss. I stomped inside and sat down at dinner mad, as the moment built to surpassing importance. Little things can still loom large when the big ones are in place.

For all Father's sternness, he and Mother were such good and decent parents, although I came to appreciate this in the oddest sort of way. Grandmother, on Mother's side, was a sweet lady, who spread serenity all throughout the house, and was fond of saying "tomatoes go with everything." Then someone asked her, "Nana, why are you always reading about autocrats and murderers?"

"Because I get so worn out, always being around such good people. I just need a little evil in my life."

As a child I was left to be carefree, especially at Grandmother's house in Culpeper, Virginia. I would drag shoes
from my grandfather's closet—his Sunday shoes, farming
shoes, rubber overshoes, town shoes, slippers, and hunting
boots—line them up, march them wildly to and fro, squeal-
ing "Shoes, Shoes," until the house shook with shoes, and
somebody barked to "tell that boy to be quiet." Okay, if
shoes were off limits, I could go watch Uncle Charles play
solitaire, or cousin Cholly sing "Streets of Laredo" on the
guitar, or Uncle Lewis milk the cows, or cousin Jane check
the grapevines, or I could pick up fallen walnuts for a quarter
(Nana's rates were always tops). It was nice being the youngest—nobody expected much from you, so go have fun.

Back then we had a housemaid named Berta whom we
loved. Father used to say that if he and Berta died on the same
day, Mother would attend Berta's funeral. Berta's grandpar-
ents had been slaves, and her parents worked a small tobacco
farm in Greenville County on Virginia's Southside. She told
me stories of how she walked through the black earth under
the sun, watching all the time for snakes, and of how her parents never let her stay past ten at Saturday night dances. Berta
liked the farm, but work in the country was scarce, so she and
her seven sisters went to the cities and found jobs. She came
to work with us when I was not yet three years old.

Berta was, quite possibly, the world's finest cook. It is a
shame that food is so perishable; Berta's belonged in a museum. She approached the kitchen much in the manner of
a chess grandmaster who knows just when to break the
rules. When she cooked, I sat at her feet. The product bore
her imprimatur. Those weren't just rolls, they were Berta's
rolls. That was Berta's crested cheese soufflé. Berta's spiced
beef, Berta's curried lamb, Berta's mushroom patties, Berta's chocolate fudge angel-food cake, those were dishes over

which Berta reigned supreme, which even the male guests glorified. Always before dinner, she'd be running back and forth, handing me tastes, talking up a storm, and I'd say, "What?"

Always I was three steps behind.

It's a tough male-dominated business, but I always thought Berta might have become a famous chef if she had wanted, but I don't know that she did. There were no questions asked back then about what blacks of any age wanted. It was assumed, silently, that everyone was happy where they were. How many gifts lay underutilized, we never had the chance to find out. Aspirations could unsettle social order; it was segregation's quiet preference to keep even prodigious talent in its place.

Berta never knew a whole lot about baseball, but she did know she was a Brooklyn Dodgers fan. Was it, I asked, because the uniforms were blue and white?

"Blue and white are beautiful," she said. But then Berta let slip into the conversation Jackie Robinson and Roy Campanella, and she was heartbroken when Campy was paralyzed from an auto accident and left unable to play the game he loved.

There being no Southern team to root for, many Richmonders flocked to the Reds, Cardinals, Senators, or even the Yankees, and Father sometimes took me to New York to watch the Gods of Pinstripe play. No one needed to explain why they weren't a Dodgers fan; it simply identified you in a way that was bad for business. Ebbets Field, the Dodgers' home, went on to become a priceless piece of Americana. Was there somewhere a white Richmonder cheering in the stands?

Fear intrudes into even the most well-off childhoods. So

much of life is new and so many things are much bigger than you are. I had a terrible fear of elevator rides: that the doors would catch with me shut inside; that the cables would snap, and the cab come crashing down; that a mean man would walk in, and there would be no place to run and hide.

Old age also can be scary. There were two kinds of faces, and those on my father's side I feared. My paternal grandfather died before I was born, but in our den was an oil portrait of him with his thin mouth and steely gaze, as if he didn't cut even the smallest creatures slack. His wife, too, was erect and stern, more handsome than beautiful, and she had called him "Mr. Wilkinson," and he called her "Miss Nellie" until the day of their marriage. Sunday after church, we visited her and two sisters, old women with wide fans in white linen dresses who pulled the shades to turn the sun to a cool but pallid yellow in their rooms.

Aunt Lilly was very old. Lilly of the dry, drooping skin. "Kiss me," she said, her eyes fastening upon me. "Kiss me." I walked up, so slowly, and I kissed her, so swiftly, lips recoiling in horror at the most token touch. "Kiss me. Kiss me," the wrinkled command of many a nightmare.

Everyone who knew Lilly said she was a nice lady. But, you see, they knew her back when. To me, she was just old. And thus blameworthy. "One day," Mother said, "you will grow old." Old? Like in college? Old? Like Mother and Father? Never, ever old like Lilly! Because, you see, Lilly was never young like me.

Lilly died one summer afternoon, and my eyes crept to the edge of the coffin, waiting for her to move. I lurched away, trembling and terrified at a face that didn't speak, see, or hear. But Berta was believable when she said Lilly went to heaven. Berta was good, and I figured she would know.

Fear is a potentially powerful social instrument. Even our fears could be used to stoke race prejudice. A rumor circulated that blacks spread polio in swimming pools. Rumors abounded too about A-bombs, which led us to stock our basements with canned goods that would keep. Then there were the sleek cars with flashy tail fins that, at least in retrospect, seemed so fashionably designed for death. Our lives were at the mercy of an errant left turn: the autos had no seat belts, the windshields shattered, and the occupants went airborne, as I almost did when my friend's treadless tires left the rainy road, with headlights silhouetting the horrifying pines, until we came mercifully to rest in a large bush. It goes to show that even the happiest childhoods are beset by fears. I was just lucky to have parents whom I knew would somehow see me through, and I worry what now happens to young boys and girls bereft of that.

Father had his own cars, which were not left to chance. A Cadillac was too ostentatious for a bank officer, a Chevy too threadbare. So he traded for new Buicks and Oldsmobiles every few years, dubious economics perhaps, but a practice that kept the public image right. Father felt almost denuded without his coat and tie, and Mother tried for years to have him remove his bank pin from the lapel of his pajamas. Silly, sure, but people drew strength from his solidity; yes, they did.

Sheltered upbringings produce a surpassing obliviousness, and mine was no exception. In the South of the 1950s, that obliviousness extended above all to matters of race. Race relations had a misguided sense of planetary order and predetermined place. The routines of childhood fended off introspection and induced benign acceptance, along with the notion that, if life was good for me, it must be equally good for everyone. Perhaps that was what made the Sixties such a jolt for some of us—that we loved all we had known, but what we knew was infinitely small.

Our smallness made it seem as though blacks in one's own city or town actually inhabited a different world. In fact, that other world had a name—"the colored section." An expression can tell its own story, and this one wasn't pretty. It implied that white was the baseline and that "colored" was some kind of deviation. Whites lived in a neighborhood, a warm, leafy place, while blacks lived in a "section" with no connotation of community at all. The term also suggests a housing apartheid, that the races were expected to live apart. But however unfortunate this unexamined phrase was generally, it must have been especially hurtful to someone like Berta, who, like many other housemaids, was at the same time so much and yet so little a part of Southern family life.

The fixedness of race was bound up in the fixedness of religion. Because my family had religion and Berta had religion, society tried to make it seem as though God himself had blessed the whole oppressive order of things. Yet faith somehow never lost its solace. I felt religion when I heard Berta sing. Mainly she sang when she was dusting; it was quiet work, which left time for hymns. They moved with her through the house like some long, sad stroke of a violin. If Berta was this side of the river, the far bank was always beautiful, and always barely in view. Her talk was sprinkled with heavenly incantations. "O, my stars," she would exclaim, when startled, and look heavenward in a hurry. Maybe heaven was a respite, a place of peace, a reunion, a chance to capture in some other world the equality that was missing on earth. Maybe, knowing Berta, it was just joy. I would never presume to say. There was the religion I learned at church, and there was the simple faith I took from Berta. At church, we discussed the meaning of the parables. What was too risky to discuss was how segregation unmasked the pulpit's pieties of human brotherhood.

Growing up is an impossible thing to do without many different kinds of love. Parental love was deep and unconditional, but it came at times with such high sets of expectations. So too did the love of teachers and mentors trying to make us better selves. Berta's love was different, because it was something separate and apart from the need to measure up. Perhaps for this very reason, Berta was the last person on earth whom I wished to disappoint.

So why, then, did Ken and I take BB guns to hunt robins, sparrows, and cardinals? The blue jays and catbirds were too tough or clever for the little BBs, and I never hit one. I once wounded a robin on the front lawn and felt a secret thrill and horror as I saw the crippled thing. But Berta was watching at the window, and she came out and bent over it. Berta could be talkative, but also quiet, as she was when she saw the wing was dragging too.

Those times I let down Berta were always worse than being punished by my parents and then forgetting the whole thing. For several years, I got a 15 cents allowance, the lowest in my class. "Don't spend it all on payday, son," Father warned each Friday. "If you buy a Coke this weekend, save the rest. You have five days left to go."

At school someone asked, "How come you only get 15 cents when my mom says your dad's got a big bank?"

Most kids in the neighborhood had yo-yos, the regular 35-cent "sleeper," the 60-cent "diamond-studded sleeper," or the 85-cent "phosphorescent diamond-studded sleeper," which glowed in the dark. I could afford only a 15-cent "beginner," which went down and up, up and down, but never

stayed down long enough to do tricks with. I couldn't stand
it. One afternoon, when Mother was out and Berta was upstairs, I snuck into the den, filched two quarters from the
stamp money on Mother's desk, and ran and bought a 60-
cent "diamond-studded sleeper." For a few beautiful hours,
I did "midnight," "walk the dog," "curtains"—all the best
yo-yo tricks. But Berta saw.

"The guys, Randy and them, gave it to me."

"Brand new?"

I suspect I knew a lot less about Berta than Berta knew
about me. We were headed one Saturday afternoon to see
her parents at the farm, and stopped at the General Store in
the vicinity for a Coke. "Thank you, Mrs. Johnson," the
clerk said at one point, and it startled me that, yes, Berta
had a last name. White children were expected to call black
adults Floyd, Big Eddie, Annie, even as we referred on pain
of death to our white elders as Mr. or Mrs. Wilson. Day after
day, month after month, year after year—there was not much
said about that.

Maybe Berta loved me because I was too young to be
part of what stained life around us. I hadn't created or defended the system, so perhaps that left us free. We lived in a
culture of many happy moments and kind gestures but also
one consumed by nostalgia for lost times and old customs,
one that was exceedingly reluctant to relinquish the old de-
grading ways. I know that Berta made my boyhood much
happier, and I like to think I brought some joy to her life too.
But I don't know how much love flourishes on such terms,
because if you admit that anything good and warm and decent goes on within a system, is that to exonerate all the
inherited injustices of the system itself? Does love inevitably
become something unequal and exploitative that the loved

one on the disadvantaged side of the equation is not free even
to discuss? Love on demeaning terms, is that the sum of it?
My childhood love for Berta had seemed only too true.

To my horror, I would not escape the system forever.
One day, Berta and I got crosswise over nothing, and I stared
at her and screamed, until those eyes welled with tears, and
I saw how deeply a black woman could feel pain. I cried all
night in my room, feeling the loss of my dear friend forever,
knowing that I'd turned as mean as the meanest white man
that Berta ever knew. I thought all night what I might say
to Berta, but there seemed nothing to say, because words
couldn't take back words. Now Berta knew. I thought I'd
get a knife and cut myself; only blood would show Berta how
sorry I was.

"I'm not like that, Berta," I said, finally, the next day.

Each September, I went to St. Christopher's, a small school
in tall pines that taught fair play. My grades there were good
enough, though Father once punished me for displeasing
marks in Classroom Behavior. But I did well in most of the
really dreaded courses, such as Miss Henderson's fifth-grade
Virginia History (where we made Civil War scrapbooks),
or Mr. Brinser's Ancient History (where I flunked but one
test—we were to sketch a Doric column and I missed the
curvature completely). By eighth grade I was halfback on
the St. Christopher's Bulldogs, right below the junior varsity.
We had terrific plays—the muddle huddle, center end, triple
reverse—and we scooted to an undefeated season.

Life just stayed sequestered. I stayed privileged, without
the burden of knowing it. Every kid, I assumed, was rather
like me. I'd never met one who wasn't. No food in the pan-
try, no clothes in the closet, no cars in the garage, no televi-
sions in the den, no country clubs, no tennis courts, no sum-

mer cottages, no wants could we conceive. And, of course, everyone went to a great school like St. Christopher's.

St. Christopher's had a student-run Honor System: No Lying, Cheating, or Stealing. It was a draconian business, with penalties up to expulsion for a first offense, but it also provided a trust as we played by the rules and believed in the Code. Early on, our class was sorted into Lees and Jacksons for many of our competitions; a suggestion that the teams be Grants and Shermans would not have been merrily received.

There were no blacks at St. Christopher's. There were no questions asked about that, either. That was the way it was, I supposed, and the way everybody wanted it to be.

When I was ten or so, big news hit: the Supreme Court wanted to put blacks and whites together in school. The politicians rebelled and shut down public schools where black children were about to walk in. Kids went to school in churches, museums, or private homes, or got no education at all. Senator Harry Byrd was said to want Governor Lindsay Almond to go to jail rather than "give in." For a young boy, it was a confusing time.

It was never just the Lost War back then. It was always the Lost Cause, a term demanding solidarity from whites even as the identity of the "cause" left blacks in little doubt.

"I'd like being in school with Berta's children," I once told a man. The smiling face turned red.

"No way, son. Virginia surrendered once. By God, not again!"

There was no talk of the Confederacy in our den, where Father and his friends got together on Sunday nights to "discuss the world." Father called me, in pajamas, and motioned me to sit on the floor. "Children should be seen and not heard," Father reminded, but he wanted me to hear, even when I did not understand.

Father's closest friends in Richmond were lifelong Virginians. There was something vastly reassuring about them; they offered stone to build a self around, character that would not crumble. Their words were soft and muted in the habit of voices that need not be raised to be heeded. They were Lewis Powell, Virginius Dabney, George Gibson—gentlemen in the true sense of being gentle men. They worked to integrate the schools, the theaters, the parks, and playgrounds. They sought to raise funds for black colleges, sponsor projects in black history, support black candidates for City Council. They also revered public peace as they revered peace and order in their own dens. Father and his friends were patient with the pace of progress. Richmond needed to be educated, not startled by a sit-in.

It was not to be. In February 1960, four black college students took seats at a segregated lunch counter in Greensboro, North Carolina. Quickly the Woolworth sit-in sparked similar protests across the South. As arrests mounted, Father and his friends despaired, their dreams of peaceful progress deluged. Our den seemed more subdued now, and Berta, too, was very quiet about it all. Father's friends could wait for tomorrow. But the language of rights is altogether here and now, and Father and his friends were living slower times.

They were well-meaning men who got caught in the middle. Faced with the Sixties, they knew not what to do. If they didn't know, how could I? Did I have to be part of this whiteness or blackness? Only grown-ups were that, and maybe being grown-up was not good. Summer evenings, when the talk in the den turned heavy, I'd run away to hideaways, maybe a thick clump of boxwood, and stare scared at the night, with its slowly crawling shadows and deep shades. That big world had problems, but kids were small enough to hide from them. How did I know why God made Berta black or me white or why it made any difference? I'd walk home, deep in thought about that, and run inside, slip up to bed, and crawl safely under the sheets. In bed I wasn't black or white, only one small kid, wondering why there was so much in this big world I could never figure out.

While there was talk of change in matters of race, it faded before the changeless patterns of my daily life. Only when change struck there, did I begin to see.

Long after segregation laws on buses were repealed, custom still held sway. One afternoon, however, the "white seats" in the front were taken. I felt silly, standing there holding a rail with all those empty seats in the back. An elderly black man sensed my plight and nodded his head as if to say, "Come, sit by me." I hesitated, weighed a lifetime of instinct, and then walked back and sat down. A few whites glared at me, the young traitor to the race. The first few minutes of the ride were torture. The next thirty, I was happy enough to have a seat.

Tennis had come into my boyhood with a funny twist. Mother took me once or twice a week to play on the coveted clay courts of the Country Club of Virginia, where she hoped I might one day become club champion. The fact that the courts were rolled and watered twice a day made them seem the very pinnacle of the tennis world, so we were shocked to learn about a Richmonder by the name of Arthur Ashe who was ascending the heights of national tennis without once playing at our little segregated enclave. Today, on Richmond's Monument Avenue, stands a statue of Ashe with a tennis racquet in one raised hand, books in the other, and a small circle of children gathered at his feet. It's a symbol of welcome change, but also of personal regret. I would like to be able to say that I had hit one ball—just one!—with the great Arthur Ashe, but I did not. From all I've heard of him, he would have spent some time to help our games. If we had let him.

I had to settle for a smaller moment. One night I was playing tennis in a public park next to a black couple. It was the first time I had done so, and I felt uneasy about that. But of course, our balls crossed each other's courts and we promptly returned them. There was a universal language to tennis, and that was that.

These were small events. By 1960, I had begun to read of a much larger world, a world which I had not known well, a South I had not suspected, a discord I had not discerned. At the State House grounds in Columbia, at the courthouse in Baton Rouge, across the South, a nonviolent voice of protest rose. A voice that spoke in placards, stomping feet and clapping hands, in high oration and in song. The mutest silence at the lunch counter spoke most eloquently of all. Single file or two abreast, holding hands or linking arms, the marchers and the demonstrators strode. "We Shall Overcome" and "We Shall Not Be Moved" were not songs with which I was familiar. I worried only that the "we" was not "me," and that the gap between my sealed world and this unfolding drama would not close soon.

To understand the Sixties, one must distinguish what came first from the decade's later years. The early moments of the civil rights movement were not only just—they were lyric and beautiful. Years later, when I ran for Congress, I went each Sunday to black church services whose cadences and resonances had been adapted to nonviolent protest. Sitting in those pews, I understood why I had been only an observer and bystander to the struggle. I offer no excuses, but my background was ever so reserved, and this moment was expressive in all the ways that I was not. History has it that the ugliness of the sheriffs and hoses and police dogs swung Northern sentiment behind the civil rights movement. That seems only half-right. The unified simplicity of the demand for simple justice; some single student face that made all humanity seem human; some word from a pulpit; some refrain from a song—I cannot tell you what it was, but that was what stuck.

I saw pictures of Martin Luther King with beads of sweat on his forehead from the swelter of long struggle—he bore the heat of the South. A face of pain, hope, patience, strength, and peace. A face of faith. A face of alien horrors, some swore, of Yankees, Kennedys, communists, and the Supreme Court. A face of turmoil at which dogs growled and hoses squirted. An earnest face that fixed the mind's eye, that never left me alone or let me forget.

"Some preacher," the young man looked up from polishing his car and spit hard in the dirt.

"Tell you somethin' son. Hope he's tight with God, 'cause he ain't long for earth."

"You want to see him shot?"

"Not sayin' I do, and not sayin' I don't." He spoke no more. The rag caressed the hood of his Plymouth. If there was love in his heart, it was lavished on that.

Suddenly, the South was under siege. The sacred South. The South of steadfast symbol, the South of resplendent equestrian dignity, the South of Traveller and of Robert E. Lee. King plowed up the old history of Bull Run and Shiloh and planted history from Selma to Montgomery: "I have a dream that one day on the red hills of Georgia . . ." the Christianity of noblesse oblige would stand aside for the Christianity of brotherhood. He led boycotts and marches and met mobs and clubs and bombs and the hatred of the smoke and flames. Amid the rubble lay not just the curse of the Cracker but the cozy world and conversation of my father's den.

"I'd like to hear him speak."

"Are you crazy, Wilk? He'd beat you bloody. He or his followers."

"Who, me?"

"Yeah, you. Especially you. You're just the kind they hate."

In history we had studied King Louis and Marie Antoinette. Inside I trembled. The teacher always told us how blind privilege tempted fate.

One teenage summer I taught at Binford, a mostly black school in midtown Richmond. The class was for remedial English, to help kids prepare for the sixth grade. Summer school was difficult. It wasn't real school, so the homework seldom got done, and teacher and pupil preferred to do what their friends were doing, which was seldom academic. Still, we made a stab at it, and by the end of the session had accepted one another rather well.

I was feeling terribly smug about having taught blacks. None of my classmates had, and I relished the thought of casually dropping into the conversation talk about my young black friends. One afternoon, I happened to be driving through a black neighborhood and pulled up at a stoplight. Suddenly I heard a call, "Hey, hey!" directed straight at me. I panicked, rolled up my window, and sweated as the stoplight turned and I squealed off, only to catch in the rearview mirror a glimpse of Claudell, one of my summer students, who had been waving and running over to say hello.

That was it—one step forward, another back. The South was messing with my mind on race, so I suppose it was good for me to go to the Lawrenceville School in New Jersey, my first long stay outside the region. I stared out the train window at a smoky, sooty stretch of seaboard—Washington, Baltimore, Wilmington, Philadelphia—and saw only strangers, people who could do without me. Secure symbols seemed so distant; my stomach had an endless drop. I wanted to run somewhere warm and sunlit to avoid the dark winter mornings and the midterm exams. I told Father I should return South for good when I finished the year, but he shook his head. When lonely, I kept company with a diary. That first winter at boarding school, I wrote a lot.

Feb. 2, 1961

Got up at 7:20 (the usual time) and went through four classes. In English we are reading *The Bridge of San Luis Rey*, which is interesting even though it is not filled with action. In Latin I proved Dr. Stevens wrong on a certain word in translation (a thing which is very rare as Dr. Stevens seldom makes even a slight mistake). Basketball was better than usual as we scrimmaged Dickinson House. We lost, but I scored two points on a long outside shot. The rest of the day I studied, watched Shakespeare's *Henry IV, Part II* on T.V., and loafed around. Supper was string beans, ham, and scalloped potatoes, the usual slop. Just as I was about to go to sleep Art came in and began twisting my arm. I got to sleep about 30 minutes later than I expected.

Only 45 more days to Spring Vacation.

I was homesick. I missed the solace that comes from being pampered, and I did not feel strong enough to fend for myself.

It was not a good thing to be shy and slight of build at boarding school, nor was it, I soon discovered, a good thing to be
from the South. I spoke that year with such an accent that a
New Jersey telephone operator asked me "to speak English."
I had much to prove—that I wasn't dumb, lazy, or a bigot.

"Now I run a loose ship here," our housemaster would
boast every so often. And "Bake" (short for Norval F. Bacon)
would flick his clipboard, clear his throat a bit, and shoot a
quick glance at his pocket watch. "Yes, as long as nobody
takes advantage of it, Griswold House will be a loose ship."
He was my favorite—a graduate of Harvard (the first man
I really knew from there), who shortly after came to Lawrenceville and spent a lifetime. He cheered the pitiful house
athletic teams, exhorted us to classroom excellence, and
humanized what he could of boarding school life. Mainly,
however, "Bake" was real relaxed. He didn't care when or
how we studied, and he never so much as blinked at passing
farts. Parents had me colliding into rules; "Bake" was always
showing me space. "Your father never went to Harvard," he
shrugged, when I mentioned it.

By senior year, I was the editor of the weekly student
newspaper, *The Lawrence*, which had a tradition of attract-
ing those who thought themselves savants; there we sought
to form a rival power center to "the jocks." We wrote with
condescension toward our "less enlightened" classmates and
drew upon our heads the furies that small questions in small
environments invoke. My own editorials urged a student
honor system such as the Southern prep schools had and, of
course, a required course on communists, who, I warned,
wished not only to terrify us with the threat of nuclear war,
"but paralyze our minds with their doctrine."

An editorial titled "Lawrenceville and Cuba" was my favorite. I had been shocked when American reconnaissance

flights uncovered the Soviet construction of ballistic missile launching sites on an island only ninety miles from the American mainland. I had listened on the radio as President Kennedy resolved to impose a naval blockade on Cuba. I tried to telephone my parents, but the circuits were hopelessly busy, and I stayed awake that night fretting that, if the country were to be blown to pieces, at least I wanted to die with my family and friends in Virginia.

The Cold War had always been an obsession. It was also an abstraction—until now. As Soviet ships moved toward the blockade, the school was swift with rumors, the main one being that Lawrenceville, situated in the "industrial heartland" of the country, would be among the first to go. Talking only terrified us all, so I slipped away, down to the three old basement rooms in Pop Hall that were the offices of *The Lawrence*. I tried to steady myself.

> We must face peril for the rest of our lives. It may subside for awhile, but it inevitably reappears in a new and more frightening light. If we flee once, we shall probably flee constantly; yet even if it were possible to free our bodies from dangers, we could never hope to free our minds from uncertainty and anxiety. . . . Panic and flight will not aid us; they only gratify the wishes of our foes and encourage their future audacity.

The crisis over, the Headmaster told everyone how brave I was. But I knew better. Bravery was a fig leaf for someone who was shaking for his life.

"Lawrenceville doesn't have a single black student," a classmate of mine protested. "Why don't you write an editorial about that?"

"I doubt that it would help."

"Why not?"

"People just aren't ready for it."

"What people?"

"Look, this school has a lot of stodgy alumni."

The problem, he said, was the paper's Southern editor, and left.

It was painful to admit that he was right. Unlike marching, writing an editorial was something I could do, but I did not. I wanted to write. But there were all those folks back home who would find out. "Hear young Wilkinson went North and took a fancy to integrate," they would whisper. So I never wrote a word. I simply lacked the courage for it, I guess.

One comes to regret such moments deeply, even well into adulthood. I knew that some were clubbed and beaten for the sake of basic rights. I knew that others found ways to rationalize their silence. Like me—why make trouble for the Headmaster, or rile the school's contributors, or cost Lawrenceville enrollment? Was that it? I could write on Cuba but not about race. Cuba didn't figure in the way I'd been brought up.

I came to love Lawrenceville. It was the green school, an oval lawn called The Circle, rimmed by quaint Tudor houses. Lawrenceville first became "past" during spring of senior year when some lower formers ran headlong into me while I was walking back from class. I flew up and shouted they should watch the hell where they were going. A few moments later, I had to laugh at my maturity. Heck, Dink Stover had gone to Lawrenceville, along with the Prodigious Hickey, The Tennessee Shad, the Gutter Pup, Lovely Mead, and Hungry Smeed, who set the Great Pancake Record. There I was, like the rest of them, ready to leave Lawrenceville and take on life.

• • •

America is a land of long journeys, of moving far from home
—to Plymouth Rock, in Conestoga wagons, to Ellis Island.
But distances are not always measurable in miles. Yale is north
of Lawrenceville. While this is a geographical fact, it is even
more a psychological fact. From my first day on campus, I
felt I traveled in a different country and listened to a different tongue. The words were nominally those I'd heard and
spoken in the South. But they were spearing instruments,
unblunted by tact.

While I traveled north, others journeyed south, toward
the source of the problem. The Freedom Riders drove the
moral message of equality through Richmond and Char-
lotte, Atlanta and Birmingham, and finally into Jackson itself.
Three civil rights workers lost their lives to bring the vote to
Mississippi blacks. At Yale, words invaded in a flurry of impatient questions, "How is it that Virginia . . . ?" To explain
was to delay, to somehow filibuster back.

At first, the violence had been that of Southern whites.
"If you have weapons, take them home," King urged. " 'Love
your enemies; bless them that curse you; pray for them that
despitefully use you.' . . . This is what we must live by. We
must meet hate with love." The power of nonviolent resistance could not withstand the welling anger of the age. By
mid-decade, black rage had swept the cities, a howl of long
oppression loosed on merchants, passersby, and occupying
armies of police. Harlem, Watts, Newark, and Detroit flared.
Urban America became a sea of smoldering walls and plun-
dered shops. The violence, when it arrived, brought no one
victory. The long, hot summers came and went, the head-
lines passed, the commissions met and opined, the frustrations
continued, the grievances did not abate. The fears intensified,
the hopes ebbed, and a nation awaited its grim fate.

With the Northern riots, race relations became not a national phenomenon, but a matter of regional recriminations. "Don't point your finger, buster," I was warned. Blacks came North fresh from segregation and from centuries of slavery. "That burden on their backs is Southern, buster. Don't ever forget."

It was impossible not to feel that America had run horribly amok. The South gloated at the North's hypocrisy. The North was more convinced than ever of racism's Southern roots. "One Nation under God," read the Pledge of Allegiance, and we still called ourselves the *United* States. But United over what? A flag spared from British bombs, only to be rent? Black against white, North against South, a nation Lincoln saved, only to be split.

During the Sixties we could not accomplish great good without inflicting great harm. So it was with civil rights. The greatest of the decade's achievements could not be wholly divorced from the decade's devotion to anger and unrest. The road from Martin Luther King, Jr., to Stokely Carmichael, from the brotherhood of man to the fist of black power—down that road is the lesson that revolutions never stop.

And this one never has. From Rodney King to Trayvon Martin to Michael Brown to Walter Scott to Freddie Gray—our powder keg is perpetually relit. Black frustrations boil over at the endless inequalities and ceaseless frisks. Motorists are fearful for their safety, and shopkeepers for their livelihoods. After every incident is the rush to choose sides. Why not await the evidence? Has there been too much history for that?

There can be no turning back. Like all revolutions, that of the Sixties opened our eyes and forced upon us the old order's complicity in the hypocrisies of inequality. Americans, save in mocking rhetoric, were not created equal. We

tell ourselves that things are better now, and they are. But
the comfort both races take in supping at the table of sweet
progress ignores the anguish of those blacks forever gazing at
the banquet from outside. They still must ask: To whom does
America belong?

Back then I thought mainly of my own dislocations. I
myself needed something to believe in, something that could
seep in, something old and durable to trust. My thoughts
turned from Yale to my state university. I wondered why I
hadn't chosen it. Since I was six, Father had brought me to
football games at the University of Virginia. He'd said how
love meant many things, including love of place. Thomas
Jefferson had worked to found the university, a fact noted
in his epitaph, and the university invariably was introduced
as "Mr. Jefferson's academic village." Father said that to live
here was "to learn at Mr. Jefferson's knee." Before the games,
we brought picnic lunches to the courtyards. Afterward, we
would stroll the Lawn at leisure, watching dusk descend on
the worn, red-brick buildings that summoned memories of
his own youth. The university went back before Jefferson, he
told me. Jefferson had modeled the Rotunda after the ancient
Roman Pantheon.

"You know when that was?"

"No, sir."

"The reign of Hadrian, as much a visionary in ancient
times as Jefferson was in colonial ones."

What Jefferson built here, I thought, would outlive all
else. He designed on these grounds majestic solitude, donated
more to the wisdom of humanity than to its knowledge.
Here were blended Rome, Greece, the Enlightenment, those
crests of civilization that peaked above its destructive floods.
The elegant symmetry of the grounds rose Mozartean in re-

finement of form, Beethovenian in grandeur of feeling. Nature itself seemed old, the tall trees taking their ease. Jefferson conquered one of the great reaches of time—the past—and taught how through the past man acquired the light to be brightened by each living generation. And yet—and yet—even this hallowed place was haunted by race. Thomas Jefferson never freed his slaves, not even those he knew and loved, not even at his death.

Still, I was grateful that I had a past, here in the South where there was infinite room for one, a past to hold onto, when everything and everyone seemed fitful and amiss. Virginia was a homing beacon when I was abroad, an anchor to my Northern drift. Home may not be perfect, but a blemished home is still a place of belonging. Whatever else home may be, at least it's you.

I remembered and, in remembering, trusted. I saw the scrawny, blue-jeaned boy of eight who acted so ridiculously grown. All my thoughts seemed to happen in summer: it was a Southern season, whose long, slow days in memory stretched over all the rest, stretched like the rural roads we drove, with red dust, rusted mailboxes, and a lonely walker, a squinting, sunburnt man in overalls with tough hands. Summer was baseball and farm stories and Berta's call to dinner—even the deaths were summer ones. The old apartments and old Lilly, everything past hollered through summer, in whose dry days life just crawled, until the night storms came and cooled. In summer we played on the shore, with shovels and sand-smeared faces by the waves. Life lasted in summer, as if I would stay eight and my brother four, and Mother always would try the waves and Father always laugh at her doing so, and Berta, too, would be just like in the picture of her on my desk. . . .

And yet the picture, of course, had long since been tucked

away, buried quietly beneath layers of sweaters in the bottom drawer of my dresser at Yale. I could not bring myself to part with it. I also dreaded someone seeing it, and having every suspicion of my backwardness confirmed. So it lay there, part of my secret life, like some prurient magazine.

It was real. I swore it. Segregation was such a rancid sore, but what happened between Berta and me was beautiful. Deep down, it was good. So why be ashamed? Why not bring the picture out? I had pictures of Mother and Father and even Eisenhower, for pete's sake. Why hide Berta's picture? She would not have done that to me.

April 4, 1968: Martin Luther King lay dead by an assassin's bullet. His courage courted death. It could have come in Montgomery or Birmingham or Atlanta or Chicago, those storm pulpits of the decade. It struck instead on the balcony of a shabby Memphis motel. It seemed different from the death of John Kennedy. I sensed fear as well as grief. "What now?" Race relations were dry tinder, ready to burst into flame.

It took his life—and death—to make racial progress possible. And perhaps it took as well the convulsion of the times in which he lived. King and the Sixties were so ironically bound—he rode the hopes of the decade, only to be consumed by its hatreds. The winner of the Nobel Peace Prize and leader of the March on Washington lay dead at the Lorraine Motel. Did the shock of his death put beyond all grasp and comprehension the bridge he built in life to move us beyond the national sin?

Biblical to the end, King praised the God who "allowed me to go up to the mountain. And I've looked over, and I've seen the Promised Land." He saw that promise in the equality of this world, not just the mercies of the next. For much of his flock, the Promised Land was not to be. For the poor, for the unlettered, for all the stragglers in old ways. Who knows what opportunity might have meant for Berta? A physician's white coat instead of the white apron of a maid?

How to sort it all out? At Yale, for the first time, I read William Styron, W. J. Cash, Robert Penn Warren, C. Vann Woodward, loving heretics in whom one sensed the Southern devotion, even as they condemned and asked for better things. The exiles carried with them a tragic sense, reminding that whatever bounties life bestowed elsewhere, in the South were always the oppressed, the starving, the ignorant, those downtrodden all their days. The exiles loved the South as a parent loves a wayward child, scolding, grieving, begging for a mend of ways. In seeking to excise the evil trait, they would cause much else to pass. "This revolution," cautioned Woodward, "has already leveled many of the old monuments of regional distinctiveness and may end eventually by erasing the very consciousness of a distinctive tradition along with the will to sustain it." But it was the only way to go. Race was inextricably interwoven with the venerable South, whose beauty and ugliness would expire one day, together, as must be the way with such things.

So it passed. One can forever debate racial progress in America and whether that whole inferno of a decade was required to achieve it. How much progress there has been lies, alas, in the eyes of the beholder. Role models inspire. We have had an African American president and there are now superb African American judges on the court on which I sit. But that may not seem like progress to African American members of the underclass, for whom housing and schooling stay so very separate. Progress is what you see around you and experience every day.

Even progress can't redeem lives lost to slavery, or the

lives of older blacks that were demeaned by segregated ways. And those whom the Southern system and its sanctioned prejudice first dehumanized, the Sixties next dismissed as "Toms" and "Jemimas," as though complaisance were some deeply personal flaw. The decade spurned such lovely, worthy lives like Berta's because they were lived before the anointed time. Progress is right for the present and future, but hard on the unprogressive past. So the housemaids of the South became a lost and forgotten generation; yet their humanity survives their circumstance and their personhood transcends the caste order America could only belatedly bring itself to condemn. And Berta must have wondered about the times in which she'd lived, and I wondered, too, about the way I was brought up. Progress makes you think that maybe you were born too soon.

I resolved for a time never to look back. Yale had already brought me some distance from the South. I determined to use that distance to begin life anew, to put behind me forever all past indignities of race. I carried out this new plan with a vengeance. I swore no longer even to think of myself as "from the South." I searched for ways not to telegraph my origins. I changed the way I spoke, especially the long "i" and that giveaway "ou." I laughed at jokes about stupid Southern sheriffs. I confirmed the tales of bigotry and backwardness. I spoke little of home, less of Father and Mother, and of Berta not at all.

"You ashamed of how we grew up?" a fellow Virginian wanted to know.

"Who can say? Home's not just where we're from but who we are."

I wasn't sure what home even means. Is home a house or a spirit? Is it even still a place? With the Internet, home is everywhere and nowhere. Communication has shed the confines of old cultures, the identifying eccentricities of the old home ways. Back in the Sixties, we sought distance from what the decade brought into disgrace. For reasons good and bad, we've been fleeing ever since.

Flight from home is one thing. But what are we running to? The question sometimes comes to me when I visit Thomas Jefferson's incomparable residence at Monticello, whose rapturous views literally preside over the endless land.

What really happened there? Were Jefferson and Sally Hemings close? Were they in love? I'm not sure how one could ever answer, because Hemings had no choice in the matter. The relationship, whatever it was, was set on Jefferson's terms. And how does one now look back on the age of segregation? Were blacks and whites sometimes close? It may have seemed and felt close, but again there was no choice. The majority race set all the terms.

The Sixties helped to strip away false closeness. Now, thankfully, there is choice, but I wonder what we've made of it. Have the races used their rightful freedoms to forge true friendships and close interracial bonds? Here and there one sees hope: friendship is natural; moments of laughter and expressions of affection now punctuate the wariness in a way they never did before. That interracial couples are becoming unremarkable is a welcome sign of change and progress too.

But, much as the shadows overtake the woods of Monticello late each day, we remain in the shadows of history. To feel history there, one must walk it at all hours; Jefferson's sunlit and shaded life demands it most of all. The Declaration's legacy of proclaimed equality is never simple, no matter what the age. The relentless accusations of racism that rose in such earnest in the 1960s have, in their harsh honesty, lent race relations a defensiveness to this day—a world of gotcha moments, of guarded conversation and hurtful connotation, hostile to the fragile hopes of friendship that persons of good will maintain today. So it becomes the easy thing to practice avoidance through a distance that cannot be bridged by White House beer summits or other well-intentioned gestures meant to heal when our separate racial worlds collide. Are we close today? Or are we still distant, albeit in a very different way?

It became hard for me to separate my advantage from my race. And so it became harder for me to believe in home as I once had. And yet good people can inhabit bad systems, and this home was mine, the only one I'd ever known. I returned from college to Virginia for the holidays, where Berta's dinners would await. One Thanksgiving evening, I drove Berta home. A heavy rain splattered the windshield, the water washing across faster than the wipers could cope. I concentrated on driving, so I scarcely heard what she was saying. It seemed to do with her work, and moments of childhood long, long ago . . .

Sometimes a single, secure thought lets a person withstand all adversity. For me that thought was always Berta. The Sixties invaded my home and Berta's, as if to mark the Civil War's centennial. How to reconstruct a home that never lost a single brick? I hardly knew, but it could not be the same between Berta and me.

I'll always love Berta. How could anyone not, so dear and beautiful she'll always be. But it's different. What was left to believe? What becomes of a boyhood in the broad, shaming daylight of the adult? What remains of a hearth that is darkened by doubt? One way or the other, the Sixties drove us all from home. At the end, in our own and separate ways, Berta and I took this journey too. But far from home meant farther from each other. The passage of time lands people in different places. And ten years can seem forever.

No one can ever defend the daily indignities of the racial world of yesteryear. The restrooms, restaurants, and water fountains bore the visible signposts of discrimination. The language bore the audible messages of hate. But it was the silences of segregation in my childhood that needed to be exposed in order to be exorcised. And when we say that race prejudice continues to exist in subtler forms, it means, sadly, that those silences continue to this day.

As I look back, I see the virtues of my boyhood as well as its wrongs. Its verities and absolutes now seem lost in time, a casualty of the 1960s to be sure, but also of the mistrust set in motion by that decade. It is one thing to believe that government has misjudged and authority has overstepped, but quite another to think that the values our forebears professed and often lived are too antiquated for our age. So duty, honor, country, character, courage, trust, and truth now seem laughably simplistic or at least less a credo for our more fast-paced and relativistic time. My home was bound up in those words, which sometimes now seem very far away. I can't live the ideals those long-ago words held up to me; no one can. But values do not become meaningless by being aspirational. And I wonder if our generation has transmitted them to those who follow as earnestly as our forebears tried to pass them on to us. I don't entirely know—it's too abstract a question—but what I do know is that our passage through the 1960s has made it a harder task.

V. The Distaste for Service

ONE BY ONE, the screen showed faces of American servicemen killed in Iraq. Name, rank, age, hometown—that was all. Different faces, so much the same. Smiling faces, saddest of all. One by one . . . in silence.

Beside each face was the silhouette of an American soldier walking toward a desert sunset. Toward a verdict of history, I suppose, that will determine whether all that sacrifice has been in vain. Events now march toward their seemingly grim fate. Was our greater error leaping in or rushing out? Neither the living nor the dead know fully at this hour. It will be a long wait.

The war in Iraq awakened memories of Vietnam. Perhaps history will always bracket the two conflicts. It would be a mistake. The Middle East is strategic; global terror is threatening in a way that Vietnam was not. Still, a president who had paid more attention to the lessons of that war would have been more attentive to the hubris of premature optimism and the dangers that protracted retail conflict in a faraway land can represent.

What we do know is how the war was waged. I'm relieved not with my son and daughter. They were both in
law school at the time. Fighting that faraway war was the last
thing on their minds or mine. That's what a volunteer army
brings, I guess: gratitude and detachment. A nagging sense
that the defense of my country has become someone else's
business. So when those courageous faces flashed before me,
I couldn't help but feel guilt.

Every now and then, someone proposes bringing back
the draft to spread things out, to equalize the burden. It won't
happen. Not just because war is too specialized or two-year
commitments too inefficient. For a draft to work, the case for
armed conflict would have to be airtight. And even then, it
might not work. The spirit of patriotic sacrifice and universal
service is not what it once was. The Sixties saw to that.

It was late at night—we had walked to the diner from a folk
concert and sat slumped in our booth, with stale, late-night
hamburgers. Betsy had enjoyed the music, and tried to con-
vince John, but it hadn't done much for him: "Just didn't
spin my wheels," he liked to say. John was depressed, certainly not because of Betsy, he hastened to add, but because
he had only just received an induction notice and here he
brought out the paper and showed me. He had thought it
over, he said, and he was going to Canada.

"Canada," I blurted. "You know what you're doing?"

He said he knew exactly what he was doing. He'd made
up his mind not to serve, but to leave the country altogether.
Things had been building up before this, he explained, but
Vietnam was it.

"Your family, your friends, your whole life, that's all.
Man, the Army's two years, after that you've got fifty."

"Yeah, but I don't think I'd care to spend them here."

The United States had become too domineering for him. "Whenever anything at all happens in this world, you can be sure America is in the thick of it. Vietnam, the Middle East, Berlin, Taiwan, Korea, Cuba—America is sucked in." He couldn't stand to be a pawn in global chess, as he was afraid he always would be, as he was in Vietnam. War had too hallowed a place in our history, he thought. "You see, for America, war has worked." We gained our independence through war, kept the country united through war, acquired Texas and California through war, kept the world "safe for democracy" in war, contained fascism and communism in war. "We'd never know when to stop fighting," he said. Our whole history had given us an incurable addiction to conflict.

"And Canada is better?"

Why, yes, certainly he thought it would be. This country was turbulent; Canada was a more laid-back place, not part of the world's polarities, though aligned with the West. "In Canada, you see, I can raise a family, work a job, enjoy my friends, and stay out of the fights. That's all I ever wanted to do, Jay, be myself and help the people around me. Why won't America let me do that, instead of dragging me across the world to kill?"

His point, more than any other, touched me. His plea was being yelled a thousand times over, in frustration, in anger, on the street corner, in the classroom, but always from the bottom of things, and the decisions were made by the deaf at the top.

"What you don't realize," he said, "is that you and I don't count anymore. I tried the whole drill, signs, marches, strikes, everything, and then one night I came back and said, 'What the hell, it's not doing any good, another 20,000 sent over this week.' I've never felt so helpless. So I thought it over, and I said Canada."

"And your family?" I repeated.

"This country was founded on people deserting their roots. It's a hard thing to do when parents love you. But like I said, we were founded by movers, when the Old World got bad. Now the U.S. is Old World in every sense, it's pushed me all against my conscience, and like the Quakers and Puritans, I'm going to move. Funny thing. I feel more like an American this way, than by going along."

Alienation was everywhere. The disillusionment of a generation with the Vietnam War ran so deep that it would take a lifetime to restore a semblance of faith in national leadership. Whether opposition to the war was a matter of idealism or fear for personal safety may be debated forever, but whatever it was, even time has found it hard to heal.

The memory of it all is fresh. It was the winter of my first year of law school, and the Johnson administration had abolished deferments for first-year graduate students. My draft board informed me that I was going around July or August. The situation called for heavy thinking soon.

The war was the pits. It poisoned every conversation. It clouded every plan. It was the dreary story that monopolized the nightly news. Some of my classmates were incredulous at the outset: how was it that America was bullying little, faraway Vietnam? I wished later I could say I'd been a moral opponent of the war before my neck was on the line. But in the early years, I was contemptuous. It was hard even to take this war seriously. It was a dirty little war that I hoped would up and go away and leave me alone.

But it didn't go away, and it didn't leave me alone, and

suddenly the suffering of the Vietnamese people seemed a matter of moral urgency. Self-interest was the great persuader. Sure, Johnson, Rusk, and McNamara had their reasons. What difference did that make? Nobody was listening to my reasons, why should I listen to their reasons? They would do what they wanted. I could throw my reasons at their reasons, but it's me that's going to die.

Lyndon Johnson's "reason" was the Domino Theory. Laos, Cambodia, Thailand, and Burma were contiguous, and small enough to seem like dominos to him. The idea was that if one fell, it would topple the others in a chain reaction. The Domino Theory was hotly debated, but whether the dominos stood or fell didn't make a bit of difference to anyone I knew. There were some things I hoped I might risk my life for, but distant dominos were not among them. I told myself that was selfish and unpatriotic. I reminded myself that some Americans were going to get killed. I asked myself why they should mostly be poor. I told myself all this and more, and then finally I told myself that one of those statistics wasn't going to be me.

I thought about death. Not that it was imminent, but that it was possible:

> *One day, perhaps, a battle*
> *Where life and death are more than musings,*
> *And I no longer a small boy snowballing the sham fort,*
> *But there exchange my martyred moment*
> *(or ill luck)*
> *For a pine box through eternity.*

I'd be damned! They weren't going to do that to me. Not over Vietnam. I'd a right to seventy years. And were the last fifty to be spent in eternity before my time? All because of one unlucky moment, after which nobody cared, because life was for the healthy and the mobile, men who laughed and carried their own weight.

I was going to emerge from this with body, mind, and life intact, and make my way from there. Thoughts came simply and clearly. I would not go to jail—it was painful in itself and a blot on the record. I would not be drafted, if that meant Vietnam. I would not go to Canada—I loved my country and had lived my life here. I could take the Army for a short time and with a safe job.

At law school that spring, panic hit everywhere. The great Maginot line of graduate deferments had crumbled. Suddenly we stood unshielded from the draft, the Army, the war, about which we had read, against which we had spoken, from which we were supposedly secure. The draft so dominated conversation that to speak of something else became irrelevant. Abruptly we were snatched from our futures—the degree, the profession, the potential unlimited. Life lay only beyond the great chasm of the Army, and the atmosphere that spring was tense with rumor.

It was everyone for himself. If the widely envied and sometimes deviously sought physical deferments were unavailable, then the next best thing was a "good program." Good programs involved a minimum of time and a maximum of safety. Navy, Air Force, and Coast Guard buildings were swamped, not because they were popular, but because they were not the Army or Marines. "I wouldn't normally give these people the time of day," someone said of the recruiters, "but now I find myself asking about their families, their hobbies, anything to up me another notch on their list." And the recruiters were visibly feeling themselves important, so flattered and befriended by the young elites. The better military options—the Air Force and Navy Officer Candidate School (OCS)—headed for an unprecedented boom. In the coveted Navy Judge Advocate General's (JAG) program, even a Rhodes Scholar might not get in.

What I really wanted was a slot in the Army Reserves. The Reserves involved only four to five months of active duty, plus one weekend meeting a month and two weeks of summer camp for the next six years. The advantages escaped no one. If you wanted to get on with life, you soon would. If you objected to the war, you probably wouldn't participate. If you didn't like jungles, you wouldn't be shipped to them. So I scoured the countryside, signing waiting lists and asking my chances. No luck. Newly created units were stampeded; in some areas lines gathered for 36 to 48 hours just to get on a waiting list.

I spent as much time on military options that spring as on law. I applied for Army ROTC, which allowed me to finish law school with a two-year obligation as a second lieutenant afterward; for Navy JAG, which also allowed me to complete law school with a four-year tour as a Navy legal officer; for Navy OCS, which would mean an immediate three and one-half years starting as an ensign; and for every Reserve unit in the state of Virginia. Each program had endless pros and cons (the safest tours of duty were seldom short), and each completely befuddled my elders who inquired, politely, how I was doing, and shrank from the alphabet soup of ROTCOCSUSAR that met their inquiries. During the day I visited recruiting offices. At night I filled out applications. I learned by heart my Social Security Number, my Selective Service Number, my father's business telephone, and my mother's maiden name. Dutifully, I told the applications what a non-communist I was, and signed my name "James H." instead of "J. Harvie" so as not to seem highbrow.

I took a battery of tests that spring, most relating to my

military I.Q. and my military personality. "Did I have a sense
of adventure?" My response was NO. "Did I like bands and
parades?" NO. Would it be fun to salute? With each answer
I kept thinking, "Now, why is it that these people want *me*?"
Maybe we'd all figure out that this was a very bad match, and
Uncle Sam, instead of pointing, would shake his head and
say, "Sorry, son, not the best idea."

My anatomy was a public product, poked at and over
in the physical exams. The idea on the physicals was to do
poorly or well; you were safer if you hit an extreme. If you
were puny enough, you got out altogether; if you were ro-
bust, you might qualify to be an officer; but if your health was
mediocre, only the draft would do. I tried to do well, because
I had no real chance to fail. My knees and back were okay,
and I had no asthma, allergies, flat feet, high blood pressure,
or sugar or albumin in the urine. The physicals were mass assembly lines, pungent with B.O., the doctors at once bored
and hurried, the shivering bodies jamming excuses from family doctors in their faces.

"You're healthy, son. Move on. O.K. Let's see, Wilkinson's the name, right, what's your problem?

"Tonsils and appendix out, measles, chicken pox, good,
wetting the bed only a childhood ailment, I presume, minor
travel sickness, feel O.K.?"

"O.K."

"O.K., next. Get up here, son."

Nothing was coming through. I called the draft board
to discover how long I had. I grew sick of things, but then a
new burst of adrenaline would come along and I would make
my rounds anew.

"Sergeant, I was hoping by May you'd have some open-
ings."

"Thought I would."

"And you don't."

"Nope."

"Any reason?"

"Just didn't."

"Well, when?"

"Looks like maybe in a couple months."

"Then I should come back in July?"

"Drop by then."

It seemed like the only hope was for outside deliverance. For a moment in that spring of 1968 our spirits soared. The McCarthy and Kennedy campaigns were riding high, the press was becoming vocal, the campuses were getting mutinous, even Congress seemed less subservient, and the enemy, which supposedly was on its last legs, staged an offensive aimed at persuading the American public there was no end in sight. "He's got to stop the war to save the country," we all said to ourselves. But while the president of Columbia was lamenting how difficult it was even to keep a university running with a war on, General Westmoreland requested another 206,000 troops; Congressman Mendel Rivers called war opponents "vermin"; General Lewis Hershey inducted those who dared to protest; King, then Kennedy, was shot; summer came and the students departed; McCarthy fizzled; and hope faded, leaving only the draft.

I didn't care to be near my friends in reserve units and hear them prattle on about their good luck. I just waited for the end. I became rude in line and behind the wheel. Waitresses must bear the full brunt of life's troubles. Some vegetable soup one night was a little cold and late, and I jumped all over the poor lady who served it.

Late one afternoon the telephone rang. It was Captain Weldon, calling to speak with James Wilkinson. "Yes, this is he."

Well, he just called to say there was an opening in his Reserve Unit, if I wanted to . . .

"You mean I'm in?"

"You're in."

"I'm in?"

"Yes."

"Wow, then I guess I'm in then." I ran off to tell somebody.

Several weeks later, I ran into John, my friend who was headed for Canada. The trip was now off.

"How come?"

"Got into Navy JAG."

Navy JAG! Safe, and respectable to boot! It should have been an occasion for the greatest celebration ever. But after the fireworks, there had come a flatness, something we both needed to talk through. So we walked a while, trying to figure why our spirits were low when the dream of so many months had finally come true. I began to sense that John was quite despondent. He couldn't believe, he said, the changes he had gone through.

When the war came, he had seen the chance to find himself. Right from the start, he had taken to the street. Protest was patriotic—it would help America find its way. He remembered one rally, when it began to rain and blow quite hard, but his commitment was such he didn't mind getting soaked. "I went home thinking I'd done a little something to help those peasants find peace."

Canada had been his moral statement. It left his personal integrity intact. "It was more than a dream, Jay. I read all about that country, and it came down to the maritime provinces or Vancouver. Somewhere near the water."

He thought his strength was such he'd never bend. "I trusted who I was. That no one could make me lift a finger for that war." Then the day grew closer and closer, and "What have I been doing? Scrambling to Navy JAG."

So there remained for us the sight of a generation running for cover. The story was a rather sad one, but it assumed worse proportions in him.

For John, what had begun as an exercise in human empathy had ended, so he felt, in a catastrophic personal defeat. Like the rest of us, he believed he had cut his private deal. For the moment, it had crushed him. What was left to be proud of? he asked. There was no sense of doing one's duty or serving one's country. No sense of anything decent or humane, either. No sense of anything, really, beyond a shameless obsession with one's own fate.

When the destructions of the Sixties are tallied, there will be a temptation to blame them all on the revolutionaries of the left. But it was never so simple. The "Establishment," which responded admirably in many ways on civil rights, misjudged dreadfully on Vietnam. And the idealism that the struggle for civil rights inspired disintegrated. The moment was squandered.

The effect of the Vietnam War on the spirits of our generation was incalculable. A fifty-year remove does little to dull the remembrance of our anger and despair. We who did not fight were doubtless pampered and affluent and all the rest, but in the end we were given nothing—at least nothing discernible—to fight for. Those who did fight were more admirable, to be sure, but military service was by and large the lost desire of the decade, and that was hardly our sole fault.

I know the counterargument. So what if Vietnam was too remote or too much of an internal struggle to justify

American intervention? One ought to enlist, even for combat, because one's country says so. As a matter of theory, I
know that to be right. But when your life is at stake, you
start asking questions, like how do you both obey the law
and stay alive?

At Lawrenceville, I had played on the soccer team with
my friend Dick Pershing, who had come there for a post-
graduate year after Exeter. Dick was a leader on the field, as
you might expect the grandson of General John J. Pershing,
the commander of the American Expeditionary Force in
World War I, to be. Dick bore his family's honor quietly and
proudly, and there was no doubt in his mind or ours where,
if war came, he would be. He went to Vietnam as a second
lieutenant, and he died there. "Wounds received while on a
combat mission when his unit came under hostile small-arms
and rocket attack while searching for remains of a missing
member of his unit," read the telegram. A wonderful man;
a terrible waste. I doubt Dick would have seen it that way,
though; his grave now lies in Arlington National Cemetery
beside that of his grandfather.

Pride in the few friends who went left a multitude of
questions for the many who remained behind. Those questions still exact a cost. Even today I do not know if I am
brave. I'd like to believe that if a different kind of war had
come along, I would have been eager to sign up and go. But
I don't really know. I did not rush to enlist, and I have not
since won a red badge for courage. Am I brave? Am I manly?
Perhaps that shouldn't matter in this very modern world, but
it does, and I don't know.

Self-preservation. That's what John said it came down
to with him. We were not true patriots. During the whole
shouting match that was Vietnam, we could not recall one
swell of emotion for the glory of the nation or the honor of

the flag. We were not patriotic pacifists either. In the end, we were untethered souls, tied to no principle that was larger than our personal safety.

The Vietnam War left many with no profound commitment to the principles for which it was fought or to the principles for which it was resisted. Finding a respectable refuge from that war was not the same thing as finding self-respect. Our destination was a personally demilitarized zone—without feeling or allegiances. "I don't ask anymore what anything should be," John said. "Whether there should be peace or war. Whether we should 'pull out' or 'stay in.' Whether America is right or wrong. There seem only things as they are, and the days as they come and go."

General Stanley McChrystal, the former head of American forces in Afghanistan, never talked to John. If he had, he might have had little enough use for him. For McChrystal is troubled by the fact that America has fought its recent wars "with less than 1 percent of the population serving in the military." He proposes a national "service year" for all eighteen- to twenty-eight-year-old Americans. Every young adult would be expected to volunteer as "a tutor or mentor in one of our country's 2.3 million classrooms, a conservation worker in one of our country's national parks or wilderness areas, an aide to one of the 1.5 million Americans who require hospice care each year or in one of numerous other areas of high unmet need."

The formidable practical problems aside, this is a noble concept. But would it be greeted today as an unfair and illegitimate imposition? "We need to support leaders who ask more of us and not those who simply promise us more," argues McChrystal. Again a luminous thought, harkening back to Kennedy's famous exhortation to "Ask not what your

country can do for you . . ." and to Lincoln's tribute at Gettysburg to those who had given "the last full measure of devotion." But modern leaders have not called upon Americans
to sacrifice, even after the tragic events of 9/11; they seem
unsure of what sacrifice entails, and they fear in their hearts
the failure of a call unheeded and a sacrifice not forthcoming.

As for a year of national service, would young Americans respond? I have no taste for generation-bashing. The
desire for service is not all lost. The spirit of the Peace Corps
lives on in projects like Teach for America or AmeriCorps,
where applications vastly exceed the number of positions.
McChrystal should be commended for attempting to re-
kindle, post-Vietnam, the embers of American patriotism. I
wish him luck. May he not find us a different and more disillusioned country. His proposal is taking head-on the Sixties
and their residue. May he not find them, even more than the
Taliban, the tougher adversary.

VI. The Passing of Unity

OF COURSE VIETNAM did not extinguish our nation's regard for the military, much less our love of country. One still sees flags all about, and, thank goodness, there are plenty of patriotic soldiers. The polls show the military among the nation's most respected institutions, but, alas, this respect is too often nurtured from a distance. We watch *American Sniper* in the multiplex matinees and on Netflix; we cheer as those incredibly brave Navy SEALs shoot Osama bin Laden in *Zero Dark Thirty*; but we know in our hearts that proximity is the measure of any relationship, and ours with the U.S. military has not been tested.

In World War II everyone was serving, married to someone serving, parent to someone serving, or working on the homefront for those serving—the war was right there among us. You could find it, people said, in the News Reels and the casualty reports. Though it was fought across the Atlantic and in the Pacific, it was a homefront war—you could feel it every single day. Could our country ever again engage in struggle on that level, where war is up close and personal and military service touches every class of person? We don't know for sure, but it's scary to guess. Maybe we could still unite, if one day we absolutely have to, maybe we could mobilize, but the Sixties generally, Vietnam in particular, and ever so much since have divided us and distanced us from military service and from each other in a profound—dare I say irrevocable?—way. Maybe whatever America needs to do, she still can do. Maybe the meaning of America can still be evoked from without and summoned from within. All of us hope, but which of us knows? To take one small example, ROTC has had a tough time gaining traction on some campuses. We think we don't need it, that we can sit back and watch technology save us, but to place our faith in drones more than in culture is a game that only fools in some false Edenic "holiday from history" would play.

Sergeant had the shortest hair I ever remember. Little stubs of hair no longer than the bristles of a toothbrush. His haircut left his ears totally exposed. In fact, it left his whole face stark, raving naked. Of course, our heads were shaved too. In less than five minutes, Uncle Sam's barber reduced us to the point where we hardly recognized ourselves. There was a difference though. Our skinned heads became symbols of humiliation; Sergeant wore his with a fierce, glowing pride.

It would, of course, have been impossible for anyone to like a sergeant. No one ever liked the teacher who assigned extra homework or the coach who ordered more push-ups. But we disliked Sergeant for a different reason—that damnable short hair.

Hair back then was the great divider of the universe. Some wore their hair square and some wore it stringy and radical. From the style of someone's hair, you could pretty well tell his views about the cosmos. In a world of "us" against "them," the enemy wore not helmets, but short hair.

It was odd, then, that the irony of a worldview based on hair eluded us. We condemned the horrible habit of dismissing fellow human beings because their skin was black. Yet our generation wrote off hundreds of thousands of Americans for no other reason than the length of their hair. We were happy enough to stereotype when it suited us. Short hairs were stamped as the most cloddish of the human breed. So we cursed them by cultivating a contrasting appearance.

That short hair let you know that Sergeant wasn't one for frills. He got down to the essentials pretty quick. We got paid $102 a month, and Sergeant explained how to make do:

"Beer an' pussy, men. That's what payday for. Pussy an' a good Falls City beer. Uncle Sam gon' take care the rest. An' men, you grab pussy, be smart an' do it 'fore payday, 'cause after, she run up prices. Men, I been in this man's Army all day, take ma word.

"One other thing, men. Only four strips o' paper for that fine rear end o' yours. Nobody here can't wipe himself wif four pieces. None o' this civilian stuff where you rip an' reel. Men, you got it easy. Back when I was doin' basic, we'd be rubbin' our holes wif weeds an' ferns, an' I catch any of you swingin' dicks usin' more than four pieces, don' come cryin', 'cause I'm gon' kick that ass o' yours till you wish it come unglued."

He was a pug of a man, vintage Army, full of swagger, out to make us men. He looked at raw recruits as though our entire prior existence was a complete and utter waste. Welcome, sissies, to a world without pity, he seemed to say. He despised civilians, "the ones who's sittin' home when we're out fightin' comm'nists," and he'd been through Nam, seen "plenty o' lead, but knew ma musket was ma friend" and that "whosever upstairs sure ain't aginst me neither."

Everyone—even we reservists—had to go through basic training. At first basic training was no more than myself and Sergeant, his being the lone presence of which I was aware. Before long, people staggered forth from his brood of glum faces and shaven heads. There was Shorty, who wisecracked: "Fuckin' with a rubber's like a shower with a raincoat on." There was Fatso—Sergeant gave the same stale nicknames to each fresh platoon.

"If I make the mortuary corps, I'll be satisfied," another fellow said. "Pop's a funeral home director, see, and I want to take over the business. Army ought to need people, I reckon, to take care of the dead. He taught me a bit about embalming, pop."

"Doesn't it bother you, spending your time around dead people?" I asked.

"Never thought much about it. Got to make a living someway. And then, who can do without funeral homes? Got to tuck 'em in decent, don't you?"

I called Sergeant "sergeant," never "sir"—"I'm no damn 'sir,' I work for ma money." To every order Sergeant appended "Be a man"—"Be a man an' scrub that thing"—masculinity meant doing what he wanted. He barked, minute after minute, day after day, and he owned you: "What the fuck you late for, huh, huh," or "Get yo shit off ma street," or "Fuck wif me an' I kick your ass" and on and on until words slung in a foul brew around his chin and shoulders.

He would walk by, eyes drifting down to my boots, snapping back to my face, and yank my unbuttoned pocket, "Hey, you shit flakey," like Durocher staring down an umpire. He loved to supervise "police calls," when we picked up trash (before daylight when we couldn't see). "Won' hear it, won' hear it," he raged if I missed a cigarette butt on the ground. Looking at him, I thought how terrible a world of only men would be, and what I'd give to see and talk with women, though the women around base became briny just like Sergeant—they acted as though they too had been through Nam.

He played by the book. Towels hung alike on beds; laundry bags tied with the same knot; bunks made with the same square corners. Deviation was a sin, except in the far right-hand corner of the bottom level of my footlocker where Army regulations stipulated "personal items." There, in the display of a few letters and a book, I exercised the sum of my discretion. I might place the book over the letters, the letters over the book, the book to the right or left of the letters, all this, and Sergeant wouldn't even care.

"Get them robes off," Sergeant screamed at me one evening when I was going to bed not in underwear, but in a pair of old pajamas. He hauled me naked to the center of the barracks, where we stood, me quaking, him seething, for what seemed forever. "No kings an' princes," he said finally. "Not in this man's Army. Kings an' princes don' cut shit. We equal, men. In the foxhole o' the Lord t'gether."

The man did have a passion for equality. In his book, equality meant uniformity. And uniformity meant dressing alike. That's why Sergeant couldn't stand pajamas. He hated "civvies" too—his word for civilian attire. If a man could dress as he pleased, he was no longer Sergeant's to indoctrinate. Sergeant's salary didn't permit much fancy wear—he took refuge in Army issue. So everything about the uniform was sacred, to be worn exactly as he said.

Basic training was long days. Sergeant's voice foghorns

through sleep, splitting our dreams. "Wake up. Git up. Up, up!"

"Oh God, I'm in the Army." The lights are on, I plunge my face in my pillow, count to ten, drag out the numbers, everyone is up and halfway dressed, Sergeant is coming, I leap from my bunk, fumble with my wall locker, a sick wave rolls over me as I think of the day ahead. Which day is it? The day for plain boots? Or for the pair with the white dot? Where is the plain pair? Aw, who cares?

I am late for formation, but I'm not seen. It is dark and bitter cold at 5:30. Sergeant is screaming, "Stop them shivers!" Off we run, the red lanterns swinging in front and behind so cars will see us, Sergeant shouting the Kill Cheer:

> *I wanna be an airborne ranger . . .*
> *I wanna live a life of danger . . .*
> *I wanna go to Vietnam . . .*
> *I wanna kill me a Charley Cong . . .*

And we yell after him, clap our hands, and run, until the stomping feet and clapping hands make the world a factory of Vulcan, smoking an air of grim enterprise. "Louder!" Sergeant shouts, but I'm silent, hating Sergeant and the song.

We stand at parade rest in chow line; it's still dark and cold and rainy. We look the same. We march the same. We sleep the same hours, eat the same mess, wear the same clothes, pack the same gear. Row upon row upon row of trainees; block upon block upon block of barracks. Sameness everywhere. "You," Sergeant bellows at me. "Why you always gotta be different? Charley eat you sideways if you dicks ain't a team."

At last inside the mess hall for breakfast, can't talk during chow, only one cup of milk, one pack of cereal, bolt from chow and again outside, in line to draw weapons, the damn weather hasn't changed. Back to the barracks, pick up ponchos, canteen, first aid pack, field pants and jacket, socks, mess gear—all here? "Clean them barracks," Sergeant screams. Sweep, mop, buff, empty, straighten, half-through and ordered to "police" the area again.

It is now 7 o'clock. The worst may be over: all is not lost because it's light. We march to the P.T. field, repeating after Sergeant:

Here we go again . . .
Marchin' down the avenue . . .
Six more weeks and we'll be through . . .
I'll be glad and so will you . . .
Am I right or wrong?
> *You're right!*

Am I coming strong?
> *You're right!*

Sound off.
> *One, two*

Once more,
> *Three, four*

Bring it on down,
> *One, two, three, four*
> *One, two . . . three, four!*

At the P.T. field, we do the "daily dozen," twelve basic exercises, each designed to tone a different muscle. Everything is "designed." Balance of diet, measures of safety, schedules of sleep, selections of exercises, issues of clothing . . . we are well cared for. Degradation through regimentation, scientifically schemed.

Sergeant points to a sawdust pit before lunch. "Always, 'fore chow, you people crawl."

"Down, geddown, geddown," Sergeant screams as we

hit the pit, slither forward, sawdust in our mouths, down our backs, trickling over the sweat. Fatso collapses and is dragged through by his belt. The rest of us stagger forth exhausted.

"Where you people going? No good, no good, git back in them pits." This time we are slow . . . one arm, other arm . . . one arm . . . other arm . . . one arm . . . we inch ahead, like half-dead mules, mouths white with mucous, dazed and nauseous . . . my hand hits the end.

After chow to the hand-to-hand combat pit. "O.K. men," Sergeant begins. "Two kinds of han' to han' fighters. The quick an' the dead. What two kinds of han' to han' fighters, men?"

"The quick and the dead," we yell back.

"Can't hear you," shouts Sergeant.

"The quick and the dead," we yell louder.

"What?" Sergeant shouts.

"The quick and the dead," we scream.

"Good. Glad you hear." We have an edge, he says, in hand-to-hand combat because we are bigger than Cong. But we must be quick. "Quick," he snaps. Then we practice the Finger Jab, Pivot Kick, Rear Strangle Take Down, Counter to the Front Body Hold, Arms Pinned. We practice in the pit, in the barracks, for "fun" until movement is instinct, and nothing remains for thought which can but fatally retard. The theory of hand-to-hand combat is to strike a soft spot on the enemy's body—eyes, throat, temples, armpits, nuts—and gouge, claw, slash, and squeeze until life leaves him or you.

During this instruction, my thoughts wander; I sift dirt in the practice pit. "You wanna fuckin' lose you life or somthin'," Sergeant shrieks at me. "I wanna tell you somthin'. Guy in Nam like you an' Charley comin'. An' his rifle jams, but he couldn' fix it 'cause he forget what they tol' him at the range. So he grab his bayonet, but he don' know how the crap to use that 'cause he sleep in bayonet class. Nex' he go to his hans but he been foolin' wi' dirt during han' to han' like you, so he plum fucked. But jus' 'fore dyin', he wish, jus' wish like shit he wus back in basic, but too late, alls they put on his stone wus 'Here Lies Didn' Try an' Didn' Care.'"

On and on he ranted. He had no grammar or diction, something he tried to cover with profanity. Day after day, words were whipped and tortured by his tongue. Many of us were insufferably smug. Illiteracy meant stupidity to us—no smart American lived off-campus, much less used his back or hands. But the gravest sin—the unforgivable sin—was to be inarticulate. We might forgive a ghetto dweller this shortcoming, but we never forgave Sergeant. He was marked by his speech as a man condemned.

Inch by inch, they tried to make us soldiers. The salute was said to be no different from the handshake, merely the military way of greeting. "Rank, discipline, duty, obedience," were all paraded by the classroom instructors. "Questions, men?" meant we could ask "How?" not "Why?" The Army taught repetition. It preached method, not reason, waging its own little war on the enemy of our minds.

We marched often to the rifle range. There we were to learn to love our weapon, our new companion, like the old hockey stick or baseball bat. Sergeant extolled the M-16: "Light as a feather. Sweet an' straight as a bird." At first I was conscious that the M-16 rifle was an instrument to kill. Sergeant could care less: "FIRE! FIRE!," he would yell, as we blasted cardboard human silhouettes that popped up 100 yards away. Once, someone got his weapon clogged with grit. Treat that thing, Sergeant said, like you would your best hunting dog.

The M-16 had a kick; I would return from the range tired
and sore-shouldered, hoping for free time. I had to look busy
on the barracks steps, so I polished my boots and belt buckle
a thousand times. Finally I would go to bed, grateful for the
passing of another day and for a few seconds of privacy before
sleep. I wondered who had slept in my old bunk before me
and where they all were now—maybe buried at Normandy
or in some soggy swamp in Vietnam. The barracks were old;
many basic trainees had come and gone. "How did D-Day
go?" I wanted to ask them, and "Did the North Koreans
really charge in waves?" But my eyes closed, I had to sleep,
Sergeant's voice would be booming, "Wake up, git up. Up,
up!" Let's see, is it the plain pair tomorrow?

I wondered if Sergeant ever thought about what his days
added up to. A teacher might see pupils go on to great things.
But Sergeant's graduates—some of them, anyway—weren't
going to live. Well, the bastard was too busy for those kinds
of thoughts. Or maybe he really didn't give a damn. He was a
perpetual-motion machine—except for one afternoon when
he came to inspect the barracks, expecting to find no one
there. He gazed a while at each bed and footlocker with the
name posted on it, but that's all he did. No oaths or utter-
ances. Just at that moment he caught my eye—it was intru-
sive to him, almost mutinous, for a trainee to catch him out
of character. The incident made him more profane for a time
and put him in one of his "scrape-ass" moods for days.

The days passed—slowly—and the Army grew old. Life
began and would end in this military monotony. A monotony of gripe and wish. It was all the same; only the past was
lively and quick, and the past was now a dream. These barracks were my reality: all I had done and could ever do was sit
day after day, making endless circular motions with the toe of

my boot. The colors grew dull—the dark green fatigues, the dirty white frame buildings, the earth of singed brown, the skies of slate gray. One afternoon, I was detailed to supply. I sat at a depot with an old staff sergeant who leaned back with his chair against the building, too hot to move, save to brush away the flies. This kept up for hours.

"Excuse me," I asked finally. "Aren't you bored?"

"Don't have time to get bored in this man's Army."

Men carry from the Army some tale of high combat, but the tellers all forget that the Army was not so wild or hazardous as it was dull. Memory has embellished this period with good or dangerous times that scarcely dented the pervading tedium. Only in the Army was I aware of time in all its components—seconds, minutes, hours, days, weeks, months, years—but the seconds moved like the last slow drops from a spigot that I shook, but the drops just hung, rested, and fell with a plop in their own good time. The slow drip of wasted days . . . that's the Army.

Uncertainties kept us edgy. We would expect weekend passes. "No good, no good," yelled Sergeant, who kept us on base. Rumors were everywhere—When was Christmas leave? When was bivouac? Who would flunk basic training? Who would go where next? All this unsettled you, or, as Sergeant put it, "fucked wif you mind." His knowledge; our ignorance—the most primitive of controls. "Think Charley tell you anythin'. Charley suprise."

The reasons we disliked him would have made our elders revere him. To them, he probably symbolized everything military experience was meant to be. Smith had served the Army decades back, lived the good life now, but had been a man when he was needed—it was people like Sergeant who let Smith age proud.

Smith had served in World War II. He did not want to die, but all young people were joining up, and he believed in his country's side. He left college for the Army and did not return for three long years. He survived every ordeal Hitler could devise. The Army and America won that war; Smith had been at the Bulge; he rode home the hero, rightly and justly steeped in pride.

Smith was not long secure. Another demon followed in the Führer's footsteps. Khrushchev led that movement, which overran from without and undermined from inside. Smith risked his life to secure the world. Let his sacrifice not die. Let America not forget the lessons of its old fascist foe. MUNICH! Give an inch, take a mile. Smith the esteemed citizen, the leading Rotarian, spoke for keeping the Army strong, urging it to little wars before they became big. "We live now in a nuclear age," he came to warn audiences, "and the communists have sworn to 'bury' us. I am not panicked, mind you, but I am concerned. What the Army needs, this country must provide."

It seems to me that our whole generation was smothered by this fear of repeating the mistakes of Munich. It was at Munich, of course, that Neville Chamberlain placated Hitler, and did much to hasten World War II. But in preaching mechanically the gospel of Munich, the World War II generation let us down. The citizen soldiers of the Second World War had fought mightily and bravely to save our country. Even more, their valor saved the world. Our generation's debt will forever surpass what we could ever repay. But the sheer depth of that formative experience led them to see Munich and appeasement everywhere. Every Vietnam was Munich. Never you mind.

A dangerous divide began to develop. We saw the Establishment—our parents' generation—as stubborn chauvinists.

They saw us as pampered, overeducated prigs. What they saw as a lack of courage, we saw as a difference between their time and ours. They fought in a war when the nation was united, and they fought for a cause that inspired personal sacrifice. What did we fight for? Ho Chi Minh was not Hitler. Ho Chi Minh had not bombed Pearl Harbor. His energies seemed focused on the legacies of French colonialism and largely within the borders of Vietnam itself. Nationalism as much as communism was at stake in this struggle. Civil war, not world domination, was at play in Vietnam. And over this, the World War II generation was preaching Munich, of all things, and the Establishment was asking us to die?

Asking us to die in a war that America had no will to win! America's leaders were incredibly replacing their formative experience of American greatness with an object lesson of how to go wrong. After Vietnam, feelings toward personal military service would never be the same. Along with so much else, the events of the Sixties managed to strain that allegiance too. With Vietnam, American government made serious misjudgments, courted a humiliating defeat, squandered the patriotic heritage of D-Day, and planted a dangerous backlash of isolationism that would endure for years. With Vietnam, the American leadership contributed to the tragedy of the 1960s. Left to right, top to bottom, blame now would know no bounds.

So off we were to go, not to serve our conscience, but to prove our courage. Off to Sergeant—the Great Maker of American Men. Off to fight the great global threat in a corner of the globe nobody'd heard of. Off to become the "heroes" of Pleiku. Off to service Smith's nostalgia. Off to repeat their rite of passage, off to any old war, thank you, Vietnam will do.

Off to death with valor, not life in fear. Off with the self that is sensitive and weak, for masculinity is the mountain of the will. Off to death by stealth, to rat-a-tats from dark, obscure foliage, to punji sticks and Bouncing Betties that strip you of your limbs. "Be yourself," I think. "Be a man! Be a man!" Sergeant shouts for Smiths everywhere, as though it were God's will.

Seventh week: We were to head into the field on bivouac. We packed our gear, marched during the day, and lobbed hand grenades. Come nightfall, the heavy marching was to begin. Already Sergeant was pacing.

Night came. Columns formed. An ambulance crawled behind to catch stragglers. Sergeant again paced the waiting ranks, "No pussies in 4th Platoon. In Nam, you drop an' you dead."

We were moving. Normally I liked marching; it left you with your thoughts. Overhead was a dusty sprinkle of stars, and the night was beautiful and clear, save in the distance where clouds girded the horizon in a vast amphitheatric sweep. Thank God, the sky could be beautiful, even over Fort Knox. I was content. The man couldn't see me now. Night marching was the most private thing of all. . . . My pack weighed 50 to 60 pounds, stuffed sloppily with mess gear, a towel, sleeping bag, shelter half, tent stakes and pole, rope, dry socks, poncho, field pants and jacket, undershirt, long underwear, ammo pouch, combat boots, razor, toothbrush, even toilet paper which, of course, I didn't need Sergeant to see. At my pistol belt were a canteen and first aid pack. In my boot was a rock, digging into my heel. As we moved, the pack grew heavier, the rock dug deeper, and I began to think I might not enjoy this particular march so much after all. . . . Sergeant was no more than a two-bit sadist, I thought. Lyndon Johnson was the one behind it: the

Army crapped on me because he said to. He's why we were marching, he's why this equipment, but Sergeant seemed to suck such pleasure from it all. . . . We moved on; I watched the man in front of me. I'd been marching with the same forty guys for more than seven weeks now. I knew them by their gaits, and I watched their packs swing and boots twist sideways over the pebbles. Why wouldn't the rock quit stinging my heel! . . . Men began to drop back now, glad I hadn't quit first, one guy was lying facedown on the trail. We were climbing a hill, bent over, the pack rolled up my back almost over my head; behind me someone's pack split, and his mess kit banged down the slope. I know, I know, Sergeant, in Nam Charley hears it, we'd all be dead. . . . The rock lodged halfway in my heel, best I could do was limp, let my left foot carry extra weight. Couldn't drop, or Sergeant would yell, "Little rock hurt you, you gon' stop, let Charley kill you, or you gon' gut it out an' live." God, let me keep going. I twisted my boot sideways, tried to shake the rock to where the skin didn't bleed. . . . Damn Sergeant, we *are* setting records, way he pushes us. Bastard said we'd break, ten minutes to the hour. I know, he don't like breaks, too hard to move afterward. Nobody has this rock in their boot, it's here, alone in the world to torment me. . . . Damn Lyndon Johnson! It's his war, his draft, his Army, his lies, his march, his rock, his pain working down to where I look it in the face, yell and scream, but only silently, the rock has forced the world wholly away from me, left me only itself, and myself, with no will, just this witless voice urging on . . . I saw us that night, from above and a distance, marching, a long column, foot soldiers in this army garrisoned across the world, Germany, Korea, Vietnam, infantrymen like me in the moonlight, the grist of great empires, Egypt, Babylon,

Assyria, Greece, Rome, England, only I carried a rifle, that made no difference, it was the moving feet that mattered; me, foot soldier; empire, American; only no one called it that, but that was my place in time. . . . Lyndon Johnson must be asleep now, home in bed with pillows at his head, nobody at home thinks of us here, he's on pillows, those big, soft white clouds he lays his head on, with the angel in them, stroking her harp to bring sweet dreams. Ha! Let strings blister her fingers, let the music screech, let the clouds and his dreams go black. Am I asleep now? No, I'm walking. Out damned rock. Even Sergeant is quiet now. I hope the bastard has a rock in his boot too.

December 6, 1968: The last day of basic training. We get a ribbon and a pep talk. That night everyone was shipping. Together eight long weeks, then scattered. "That's the Army," someone said.

"All for Gordon, Benning," Sergeant shouted at 11 P.M.

"Lee, Belvoir, George Meade," he yelled at midnight. The ones going to these posts were lucky. They probably would not learn a combat skill.

Groups of two or three filed into the night, dragging their duffels.

"Men for Bliss . . . Fort Sam (short for Sam Houston and the Army Medical Center) . . . Sill (artillery) . . . Bragg (Airborne, a scorched plot of sand and pine trees) . . . Dix . . . Ben Harrison (finance, journalism maybe, they really were fortunate) . . ." It was now 3 A.M.

"Fort Polk." There was silence. "Fort Polk," Sergeant shouted again. He was a prison guard calling death row. Fort Polk, Louisiana, was infantry school, last stop before Nam. The Army called it "little Nam," because it was swampy and overgrown, and even had punji sticks like Charley used.

"Men for Polk git a move on," Sergeant shouted.

The fellow who wanted the mortuary corps had been assigned to infantry at Fort Polk. For me, if I were lucky, basic
training was the end, for him only the beginning. I could not
face him. I lay in bed, pretended sleep, prayed he would not
wake me to say good-bye.

I heard him gather his things. Slowly. He had known his
orders were for Polk a week ago, but it would hit him hardest
now. His father had come to see him. "It's a sad thing, they
do your only child like this," his pop said.

"Move along now," Sergeant said. The boy hardly heard.
What more, after all, could they do?

Somewhere, back in basic, I had been crawling through
that sawdust pit before chow, sweating to make it, when I
suddenly stopped and half sat up, thinking, "What in the hell
have we done to deserve this?" The Army was surely a punishment for something, though I did not know what. Now
as I heard him start to leave for Polk, it dawned on me. What
in the hell had *he* done to deserve it? Sure, I'd heard the patriotic speeches: that's why he was going. But why him? He
wrote his folks; he said his prayers; he shared his canteen. I
lifted my eye very slightly from the bunk to see him. His face
was futureless. He was walking away. Just another statistic,
another possible little digit of death, for the Army to chalk up
and shrug away. Hell, it happened all the time.

I could think of but one thing that night. That I'd never
see Sergeant again. Come tomorrow, the man would be
gone from my life for good. I was sure he resented me. I had,
I supposed, made his life as miserable as he had made mine.

Over time I came to believe it might be less his fault than
mine. Sergeant never stood a chance with me. I disliked how
he looked. I disliked what he wore. I disdained the way he

talked. I distrusted what he thought. Above all, I detested
what he symbolized. Somehow he came to represent all the
barking dogs of war and the howling winds of national aggression. He loomed before me each morning in the barracks
as the pawn of those who plotted our untimely deaths.

The war in Vietnam was wrong. But how had all the
evils of that war come to rest on this man's shoulders? What
had *he* done? Made me crawl through one too many pits?
Shoot one too many rounds? March one too many miles?
Thrust one too many bayonets? It was one thing to fume at
what Sergeant did. But the passions of the time required that
we despise not who a person was or what he did, but what
he symbolized. So I came to hate a man whose only sin was
trying too hard to save my life.

For days upon days, I assumed this man, so belligerently
bald, had nothing—absolutely nothing—to say to me. So I
made of him cold matter, as I had of countless others whose
manner stripped them of all claim to personhood. I understand now how people come to be purged as people in the
minds of their antagonists—maybe that's what social struggle
is about. People often weren't people in the Sixties—only
symbols of this side or that. During that decade, more Americans annihilated fellow citizens in their consciousness than
were slain on the field of any battle.

Nowhere was this more true than of Americans in uniform. It became for the Sixties the most sinister of suits. Society put its pigeons in uniform. When the state commanded
"Fire," those in uniform always fired, no difference what target, no matter what cost. The dissidents of the Sixties had a
word for those in uniform—"pigs"—crude, filthy, snorting
louts. Were uniforms necessary to a modicum of social order?
No, Sergeant wore the raiment of raw oppression—of that
we had no doubt.

How sad that the decade that so rightly opened its heart to many, so promptly closed its heart to many more. It didn't matter whether the wearer of the uniform was a policeman or a fireman or a sergeant or what have you—they were seen as bigoted, conformist lackeys all. Soon enough, the short-haired and hard-hatted sensed that class prejudice had simply been substituted for race hatred, and the political consequences for 1972 and 1980 and beyond would be profound. But Bull Connor's vicious dogs in Birmingham and the billy clubs of the Chicago police made us write off other honorable and decent folks in uniform as not deserving of respect or hardly worth our while. Even now, even after all the bravery shown on 9/11 and its long military aftermath, I doubt that we who came of age in the Sixties will ever fully value what our fellow citizens in uniform do. We may honor soldiers, but largely from afar. And even today police are written off wholesale in street protests, stripped of their humanity by uniforms the Sixties saw as uniformly bad, no matter what good their wearers might upon occasion do.

The wounds from that war cut ever deeper. Vietnam and the Sixties made America a more selfish nation than it had been before. To be sure, we have always had divided opinions and weariness in our country during wartime, the Revolution and the Civil War being prime examples. And democracy is a system designed to mediate discord. But by going to war in Vietnam in such misguided circumstances, the government created a "me first" opposition on a scale not seen before.

Vietnam also fractured our notions of national unity in times of war to an extent that may one day put us in real danger. The war did have the salutary effect of encouraging more debate about the wisdom of our country's foreign military endeavors. But Vietnam made common bonding during

foreign conflict immeasurably more difficult to achieve—
witness the dissolution of our fleeting shock-induced camaraderie in the aftermath of the Pentagon and World Trade
Center attacks. The folly of Vietnam gave hope to enemies
everywhere that they could wait America out, that they
could turn opinion at home more easily than the tide of battle abroad. Patience is not the strong suit of a democracy to
begin with. If we turn so impatient with each other, will we
show patience overseas?

Like presidents, wars acquire reputations over time. And
the respect, even reverence, we pay veterans seems to rise
or fall with the reputation of the war in which they fought.
It has been my privilege to know men, now deceased or
in their nineties, who fought with the 29th Infantry Division on Omaha Beach, or in the Solomons, or on Okinawa.
If military service in World War II led some like Smith to
boastfulness, it led others to long silences. "What was it like?"
I wished to ask. But I never did. Their silence, out of respect
for fallen comrades, made them more heroic still.

We seldom ask those who fought in Vietnam, "What
was it like?" We don't really wish to know. Those Vietnam
vets who were exemplars of courage every bit as much as
their World War II forebears now slip quietly out of national
consciousness. It remains difficult to commemorate what we
once deplored. It is the final cruelty of that war.

A colleague of mine on the court from North Carolina
fought valiantly as a young first lieutenant at the Battle of the
Bulge. His infantry unit spotted four German tanks coming
over the crest of a nearby hill. The men through grit and
pluck had managed to survive, and every year after the war
my colleague and his first sergeant made it a point to get
together, until the old sergeant died. My friend is a judge of

refinement and intellect; his first sergeant was a man of his hands. They lived throughout in mutual respect. As much as Vietnam brought divisions, their war created bonds.

Where are those bonds now? The toxic stew of the 2016 election has many causes, but the contempt with which the young elites of the Sixties dismissed the contributions of America's working classes was surely among them. It was left to demagogues to stir the resulting resentment to the point that Americans now not only demonize difference but flee it. We see today Americans seeking to live and work with people like themselves. To an extent that's human nature, but at some point sub-cultures begin to predominate and the power of our unifying symbols fades. We become others to ourselves. Our wars become something "someone else" is fighting, though the "others" are our fellow citizens. So much of our otherness began in the 1960s, though in the loss of mutual respect and national community we have all since been complicit. Have we now reached a point of no return, where we cannot unite again?

History abounds with doomsayers, those whose specialty is grim reminders and dire forecasts. Cassandra, the ancient prophetess of Troy, spurned the advances of the god Apollo and was condemned, so the story goes, to never having her prophesies believed. Elijah, the great Hebrew prophet, inveighed against the worship of false gods. Winston Churchill railed against the rearmament of Germany and the existential threat to Great Britain and the West. But even the prime minister's majestic thunderings may not be the American way. Roosevelt and Reagan helped light a path of joy to penetrate dark periods, and American exceptionalism must mean irrepressible hope as much as it means anything. When I see my grandson fall back laughing in a bin of colored bubbles,

I wish to leave him not Sixties gloom and division, but the hope that understanding how we came to make such enemies of fellow citizens can lead to some more harmonious day.

I played my own small part in those divisions. I remember when it came my turn to depart basic training. As a reservist, I was going nowhere dramatic like Fort Polk. In fact, I would become what the Army called a "personnel specialist" (really a glorified typist), and my training waited at the other end of Fort Knox. I stood, waiting for the bus to drive me away from basic, away from 4th Platoon, when Sergeant approached.

"Well," he said, almost softly. "Good marchin'."

I said nothing. I stared straight ahead. A moment passed, and he walked off.

I've regretted that. So many times. I recalled the scene often, and pretended I had spoken, or mumbled, or even nodded. I wondered what happened to him, whether he returned to Nam, whether he was still alive. Of course he was—the guy was charmed. What did he make of my silence? "You think I hate you, Sergeant. That's what you think. You wrong, Sergeant, you wrong." And one day I thought I'd call to tell him that, but how would I find him?

Sergeant . . . I can't recall his name.

VII. The
Fall
of
Faith

IN THE END, when all else had been leveled, the 1960s went after God.

My first sight of God was in flowing purple robes upon a swing. I think He wore purple, because He was king. He swung because that was something anyone would like to do.

Nobody ever told me God looked that way. I just knew.

Prayers were another way of staying up late. Grown-ups talked to me, and read to me, and tucked me in tight. "But you forgot to say my prayers," I said, just when they thought they were all through. "Now I Lay Me Down to Sleep" was not a long prayer—only four lines—but at the end I asked God to bless every friend and family member I ever knew. "I know I haven't seen Aunt Deborah in years, but God bless her too."

I hope God didn't mind my using prayers that way. It's just that with grown-ups, being devout was foolproof.

Church, I thought, was a child's place of punishment. It was even placed, diabolically, in the middle of the weekend.

It was there we paid our respects to monotony, there that sermons taught us to endure, there we learned that squirming was to sin in God's sight. For the messy room, for the naughty words, for making life so miserable all about the house, I atoned where else but in church. "We have left undone those things which we ought to have done," the voice droned, "and we have done those things which we ought not to have done; and there is no health in us."

"What's that mean?" my brother nudged me.

"It means you have been evil," I replied.

Sunday school classes were better. There we could move about and talk. Once, we sat and read religious comic strips. There was something unsettling about reducing holy tales to the same medium as Blondie, but hrrmph, it was approved. Who wouldn't remember the Lord parting the Red Sea waves, the Israelites crossing in the nick of time, the Pharaoh's horses and chariots swooshed away by the avenging seas? The Bible was great stuff. When David slew Goliath, there was hope for neighborhood runts everywhere.

I once sought heavenly advice on a weighty matter: tobacco. Virginia was a tobacco state; smoking seemed the patriotic thing to do. The oldest guys at school belonged to the Smoking Club. Many of them wore varsity letters too. Then one of my cousins called it dirty, filthy, and disgusting, and said she'd rather kiss someone with donkey breath. I thought I'd let God resolve the question.

The minister chuckled. "Does God permit smoking?"

"He won't say."

"Well, I admit, God can be very ornery. When I was young, I asked God whether it was all right to ride an airplane. Some people thought them a little too near heaven, you know."

"Well!" I asked. "Did He say?"

"He was always glad you asked the question. But He never answered a thing."

And yet there were answers in religion. Right was right, wrong was wrong, and in the flourish of duty, honor, country, it hardly seemed fitting to leave the Lord in doubt. Father was resolute about religion. A vestryman could be trusted as a businessman too. God struck an image of paternal authority. No doubt, I used to think, He sat at the head of heaven's table too.

Mother, for her part, loved the rhythms of the church year. For weeks, she would look forward to "Welcome, Happy Morning" on Easter Sunday. "Well, why don't you sing it right here and now?" I asked, which brought smiles, because a congregation was needed to protect Mother's high notes. The psalms and prayers appealed to Mother as literature. Poinsettias on the altar warmed her aesthetic sense. "One can have faith," she told me, "and still find in church satisfactions not strictly religious."

One thing was certain: God smiled on my country, on my parents, and on me. America was God's land. The Lord, as the song said, "shed His grace on thee." Our church was God's house; our congregation God's guests; our service a kind of special conversation, reserved for "thou" and "thee."

The bounty of our lives was a sign of God's blessing. You could look at folks back then and tell where they were headed. When Mr. and Mrs. Warwick walked the aisle each Sunday to their pew, when Mr. Keith passed the silver offertory plate, when Mrs. Alexander, the soprano, sang "Come, Labor On," you knew where they were destined, you absolutely knew. These were people to praise, their lives tablets of virtue.

But then the minister would read, "If thou wilt be perfect, go and sell that thou hast, and give to the poor, and thou shalt have treasure in heaven: and come and follow me." There was a stir, a breath of restlessness, even from adults, as everyone waited, expectantly, to learn why the Bible was not a literal text. For the moment, my new sailor suit was on the line, Mother's new slipcovers, even Father's new Oldsmobile. Later, I learned that was the sermon affluent congregations always had to sweat—the "gotcha" sermon, a friend liked to say.

There were things about God there was no escaping, not even in a brand-new sailor suit. There were times to settle up. "For unto whomsoever much is given, of him shall be much required." Perhaps because of that, faith at home was very private, a subject one would never yammer on about. Each Sunday morning, we worshipped with what seemed like a multitude. Yet one lived with one's own thoughts.

If faith was private, so too was sin. I got the knack of it quite early. There was a boy in school named Carter who was unpopular because he was awkward, with limbs to baffle a puppeteer. He would ask me to his house each Wednesday afternoon, and I would go because of his color television set, electric trains, and trampoline. Carter always wanted to be part of our touch football games. One afternoon, there were nine of us, one more than was needed for two teams of four. If I were captain, Carter would expect me to choose him. And we would lose. So I chose Jerry, Mark, and Joe.

I realized that night that God could read thoughts. No parent could do that, not even a friend. But God understood how I'd done Carter in. Thoughts were impossible to clean up, to make pretty. So I would sit and ruminate: Now who let God in? He was impossibly intimate. If I thought about sex, why God would know. If I fudged at cards . . . if I lied to a friend . . . if I complimented Mother to ply money out of Father, drat it, every complex connivance came under God's gaze. I saw heaven as hopeless, God leaving no hiding place for sin.

Even things that pleased Father didn't always thrill God. Like getting good grades. And God didn't much care either for a winning football team.

"It's unfair," I said. "Why won't God approve the things that mean the most?"

The minister thought we had enough applause without God chiming in.

"Why do you put up with God?" I asked him.

"Of course, I hide too," smiled the minister. "At heart, we're all fugitives. But why flee from a friend?"

God was a friend. Many summers ago, when the family was vacationing at Woodberry Forest, God must have come along too. Woodberry lay somnolent in the Virginia foot-hills, the kind of place where nothing could go wrong. But Mother and Father were walking toward the car one morn-ing when I did what I'd been warned never to do: jump in the Woodberry swimming pool. Down, down I plunged, then up choking with water, gasping for air, then down again, up, down, down to drown, I was sure, when I sent up a frantic prayer. A Woodberry student saw me from the diving board and jumped in and saved me. I had not thought anyone was around. That evening, I prayed an extra amount and promised God never to disturb Him on such short notice again.

The day after Christmas, five bodies were carted from the charred ruins of a home. The culprit: a cigarette left on a sofa. My friend Foster never smoked; he was not to blame. Family members were found near the window, by the closet, in the bed. Had someone a second to pray?

Why Foster? This time the minister shook his head.

"Without mystery, there is no faith."

But Foster was dead.

Like everyone else, I wondered whether there really was a God. There were churches everywhere. All Richmond went to worship. That was proof, was it not? The whole population of Richmond, Virginia, would not be doing a ridiculous thing. Mother said that God was everywhere: in the flowers, in the trees, in the lakes, in the mountains, in the love one could not see but feel, in the breeze. The truth is, I myself wanted badly to believe. The surest way to provoke God's wrath was to doubt His existence. Faith was, I suppose, partly a matter of improving my chances.

Away from home it was easy to slip out of the habit. We had compulsory chapel at Lawrenceville, but the service was so secular it seemed more like class than church. At Yale, little was compulsory at all. Late Saturday nights made it hard to get out of bed on Sunday mornings. Sleeping late didn't mean you were an atheist, but the observances encouraged by college life were not those of faith.

Yet my faith survived. It withstood not just discussions of evolution but even the space age—though a course in astronomy gave me pause. I tried to pinpoint myself: in a home, on a street, in a city, in a state, in a country, on a planet, in a solar system, in a galaxy, in a universe with billions of galaxies, each with billions of suns, and I asked, with all that out there, what time has God for me? It had seemed to me, as a boy, that God had infinite patience and time. Too much time, so well informed He was. That had been my belief— that God was close to me. Now I wasn't sure where He was or even who He was—I knew only that He was not above those white fluffy clouds on a swing.

God has been hammered ever since the Enlightenment, whose philosophes exalted reason and disdained the superstitions and dogmas of the old religious world. The collections of a great museum are segmented into periods, and it's quite a journey from Raphael's rich, exquisite reverence for the sacred to van Gogh, Cézanne, and Picasso, whose dazzling talent didn't seem, to my untutored eye, to take much account of God at all. In a sense, God remains the great victim of modernity, and no doubt He would have taken a beating had the Sixties never come along. It's just that the decade gave Him another rude push. The Sixties with its insistent presentism that focused so supremely on the moment left little time for awe or contemplation of where we might have come from or where we all shall go. Americans have always been a religious people, and in so many ways we still are. But I suspect we are a less religious people as a result of living through the 1960s. In my own case at least, the challenge to my faith was profound.

No doubt Einstein and Darwin posed a more serious challenge to religious faith than the 1960s did. But in one sense it was easier to reconcile God with the laws of physical and biological science than with the conditions of human beings. The former was rational and majestic, consistent with the hand of the Creator. The latter was random and inexplicably sad. The black voids of interstellar space made more sense than the back streets of Bombay and Calcutta, with their clots of wasting bodies, the flesh too lean for vultures, the eyes hopeless in the head. God may have made us in His image, but He left us to our fates. You look at Scarsdale and believe, but look at Watts—is God now dead?

It was not the questions of the Book of Job that were res-
urrected in the 1960s. In Job, at least, one could observe virtue being tested. No, the question was what Edwin Markham
had posed in "The Man With the Hoe":

> *Bowed by the weight of centuries he leans*
> *Upon his hoe and gazes on the ground,*
> *The emptiness of ages in his face,*
> *And on his back the burden of the world.*
> . . . .
>
> *Is this the Thing the Lord God made and gave*
> *To have dominion over sea and land;*
> *To trace the stars and search the heavens for power;*
> *To feel the passion of Eternity?*

Late one spring, I attended a forum on religious values.
I almost decided not to go. I won't forget what I heard:
One cannot witness the despair in our world without asking, where is God? If God is alive, asked the speaker, why
was Martin Luther King dead? Why had Robert Kennedy
been shot? If God is alive, why were American bombs dropping on Haiphong? Why was racism rampant in this country and throughout the world? Why were slums and ghettos
spreading? Why did Biafran children starve? Why was mankind stockpiling arms for Armageddon? When would nuclear
blasts blot out the sun? There was no way, he insisted, to
reconcile such things with God.

On May 4, 1970, students at Kent State protested their
country's slaughter of peasants in Cambodia. Their demonstration proved too much for Governor Gilligan. The National Guard gunned them down. Four dead students, our
age, became markers of the chaos and mindlessness and god-
lessness of our time.

Bells tolled. Temporal authority had been discredited. Now God? What yet matters? So we favor civil rights, that does not matter. So we oppose the war, that does not matter. So we are right or wrong, good or bad, kind or callous, that does not matter. In the days of Dante's Hell, it mattered; now we are one by one laid to indifferent rest. We need God to matter. We need faith. No, they say, God is dead, just look at the death besetting the world. If King and the Kennedys, Vietnam and Cambodia, if this decade of untimely deaths really does mean the death of God, what is left to do?

Throwing God into doubt left some less and less to live for. I recall a college friend, who had lived on the edge, motorcycle fast. He took a leaf, tossed it to the wind, watched it eddy and dive. "People," he laughed. "We're like that leaf. After thirty, we begin our descent. A little gust may hold us up a moment. A final twirl, and then we die."

What, he asked, does life hold but death at middle age, when we shape selfhood to fit a status, when we crave others' approval on ladders to a mocking sky? When all we want is money to join the club, success to still the gossip, vice to flee the tedium . . . "Wait!" I shouted, with David revving his cycle, streaking life's last hours by.

The Sixties seemed to offer no life after death. No middle age. No life after tomorrow. No yesterdays. Only here and now, this compressed second, running on fumes. Time sliced from both ends, to this screaming instant, this frantic sliver of sensation, for someone to shoot up and screech off in.

I imagined an outpouring of hundreds, even thousands, gathering before the ghost of Woody Guthrie, bewailing America's state. "Read it! Read all about it!" cried the Jeremiahs on the corner, waving the country's corruptness in our face. They were packing now, provisioning like Noahs before floods rained down the national disgrace. Reform had been to no avail; the only recourse now escape. "Look not back," the Sixties warned, "lest we be consumed in Sodom's fate."

"Wait!" I yell. "The sin is not so great. America is good— let me tell you of my faith. She has to be good, there is such beauty to her names, Mississippi, Shenandoah, every time you say those names they sing, Virginia, hymn to the plumed past, Oregon, born of woodland melody. Sing, sing of free-ways, superjets, smartphones, and satellites, sing science and invention and medical discovery. Sing to immigrants and presidents, to the Statue in the harbor, to Rushmorean maj-esty. Sing of Yorktown, Gettysburg, D-Day and Midway, of Lincoln and King and Susan B. Anthony, sing, sing forever: praise her vitality."

"No! What she was, she was only in myth. Sing, rather, to her reality. Sing of Newark and Watts, of Ferguson and Baltimore, of My Lai and Abu Ghraib. Sing while jagged scrapers hack the sky to gloomy patches. Sing of car fumes, of dead fish by lakes, of dust on dying miners' lungs, of Indians besotted by the white man's drink. Sing, sing of Mrs. Cabot, the capitalist's bride, obese rings squatting on slender fingers, sing of migrant labor foremen lashing the last spent shifts. Sing, sing of bondage in the Land of Liberty."

"Wait!" I cry. "Where would you go? What Arcadia awaits? Look here. More justice in law, more democracy in politics, more opportunity in business, more creativity in sci-ence, more freedom in religion than any place on earth."

But the crowds had left my dreams long since, so shaken was their faith.

After the Sixties all that was left in me were questions. "America, what are you? I no longer know. I hear only your myth makers and your myth destroyers, they don't care about you. . . . What were you, before people gave up loving you to loathe each other, speak to me and tell me what you are. But you seem only my magnified confusion. Don't you know where you're going either?

"You thrash and curse and smite yourself, leaving only your sores for history to see. Let it see you, then, not as a sainted nation, nor as one that sinned, but as one that tried. Not the nation that overcame bigotry, but that strove to. Not the nation that gave the planet peace, but that wanted to. Let it see errors of judgment, but not hardness of soul. To achieve peace, abolish poverty, approach justice, those were no easy utopias, and all disputed how to get there. The disputes were harsh, the utopia stayed misty and distant, but still you never gave up on it. America, let history say you were a nation that tried."

What I wanted was an end. An end to it all. My brother, Lewis, was a fine photographer. He took pictures to find peace. Maybe the shots were of sunlight on trees, of shadows on mountains, or of Webster, his Irish Setter—whatever the photos were, they were still.

And will stillness ever settle on the Sixties? What sort of past will we make? Were we a concerned and compassionate generation, or a horde of strident fools who did not laugh near enough, and as we passed left but a bitter taste? And when the darkness falls upon our shouts, how shallow might we seem—will someone ask: "How did these students manage to say they were maligned?" And if that someone saw evicted deans and shattered windows he would think, "They were as wrong as the war they tried to stop." Who will honor us? We did not honor old age—we honored no age but our own youth. We gave no credence to either heritage or history—we said only what a mess it made. *Ruhn in Frieden, alle Seelen*—All souls, rest in peace—will no one pray that for us? Because to the past we paid no quiet homage; we were only *enragé*.

How will we see ourselves? "Most of us cared," we may now say to our grandchildren. "Much was wrong at the time, and we saw that and tried to help. We had half a million men fighting in a little piece of land you never heard of, but that's a long story. You may find it hard to believe how it was back then, Lisa, but black citizens in our country couldn't get into white schools, or restaurants, or buy a house in white neighborhoods, and they were pushed and packed together in the most dismal parts of town. As a woman, Lisa, you would not have been free to develop your gifts and find out who you are. We were students then in college, and we were all upset, so upset over so much wrong that we did some very foolish things."

"Are you sorry you did them, Grandpa?"

"No, I don't think so."

"Then why are you so sad?"

But perhaps the lecture will proceed like this: "It was the time of the angry student putsch to utopia. It burned itself out, because there was no tolerance, no gentleness, only heated glares. At its pinnacle of power, the nation became afflicted by a new nemesis, self-loathing. It was a virtuous nation, all things considered, but it became nauseous with a feeling of wrongdoing, a sickness born of intense guilt that the country's affluent students brought to bear. Through this somewhat obsessive wave of condemnation, the country lost cohesion, its sense of shared values. We read of pitched battles between white and black, young and old, that tore at the national fabric almost as much as the great Civil War of

one hundred years before. What the two World Wars did
to the British, these students managed to do to the United
States. Rigid prejudices were challenged, but so were religious, patriotic, and familial values, which, however pietistic,
formed the great sinews of national strength. The early empires, you will remember, fell at least partly from without,
but America exemplifies most clearly the later trend of great
powers collapsing without clear external cause."

I thought blue and gray the last colors to describe two
Americas. But red and blue now seem part of two very different flags. The two Americas embrace divergent narratives.
Red America would restore those values that the Sixties
stole away; Blue America seeks to protect the Sixties' gains.
Red America invokes an idyllic life before the 1960s—when
respect for families and parenthood reigned, when religion
existed as a guide to larger meaning, and character formed
the gateway to a worthy life. Red America seeks salvation in
community, institutions, authority, and symbols, be they the
Pledge or the pulpit or the flag.

Blue America is more apt to see in this salvation the return of intolerance, a rejection of modernity, a refusal to recognize that patriotism can take many forms, even that of dis-
sent. Where one nation sees community and faith, the other
sees repressive orthodoxy at odds with democratic pluralism,
at war with scientific method and medical research. What
Red America views as permissiveness, Blue America sees as
personal freedom, a value to be cherished in the most intimate choices we make. While Red America sees the source
of evil in the 1960s, Blue America sees the roots of wrong in
the decade the Sixties sought to replace.

On and on the conflict rolls. The Sixties encouraged us
to fight such domestic differences to the death, to square off

in opposing camps and armies, to slay the religious right as zealots or the secular left as infidels. So both Americas have turned intolerant, just as the Sixties taught us to be. We strike our mutual blows as though our nation were exempt from history's laws and reckonings, as though it wouldn't even matter what one day happens from abroad so long as enemies at home are suitably debased.

I had no way of knowing at the time that any of this would come to pass. I did sense something most disquieting had happened, and I wanted only to become the person I once knew. We see ourselves in mirrors all our lives and wonder: must these changed external features mark interior revolutions too? Maybe the time had come to awake from these alien years. I had, after all, been raised to be pounded by heresy, and to pop back into shape. Didn't we all have childhood as our baseline? There the constellations were set, the values which we navigate life by. There was found the refuge from the squall. There imagination first took hold. Memory never relinquished those years, and the intervening time was but an interlude. There were childhoods of broken homes and bruised bodies, of neglect and indifference, but mine was different, serenely so, a childhood that would never lose its hold.

But it had. Shortly before graduating from law school, I met two old family friends at Richmond's Commonwealth Club for lunch. The Commonwealth had done what many clubs tried to do: age gracefully. It was as I remembered: the long, canopied entrance, the portraits of Confederate generals in dress gray with red sash and saber, the lounge, the ballroom, the spiral stairs ascending to a private dining room, where we lunched over an array of silver and mint linen.

The friends, senior partners at a splendid Richmond law

firm, offered a flattering salary, my choice of field, anything a fledgling lawyer might think to ask for. Their firm had established clients, a challenging practice, a discreet blend of professional quality and social standing. Their offer was, you might say, a ticket to a gracious home, privileged offspring, exclusive clubs, deluxe vacations—to a life warmed by the brandy of respectability. That prospect, in turn, warmed Father. One thing he never said and never needed to: I was not his namesake for nothing.

I did not accept their offer. I knew in the end that I could not accept it. Ten years earlier I would have grabbed it. But too much now separated home and me. It was not a separation I welcomed. But there it was—all the dissonant chords of a decade that could not convert, but did estrange.

The experience of the 1960s left the calendar but stayed within me. I hoped that futile wars might be fewer, and that Berta's descendants might be truly free. I hoped that conformity would not break the nonconformist, and that government would not desert the dispossessed. I hoped that America might profit from the Sixties, but I prayed that it would never have to live their like again.

For all its eventfulness, life in that decade left the deepest loneliness. Life does draw meaning from something "more than me": from the family that nourishes us, the school that educates us, the community that welcomes us, the conventions that guide us, the laws that govern us, the patriotism that inspires us, and the faith that sustains us. All these forces were weakened in the 1960s, and the individuals depending on them were in the end wounded too. In the 1960s, America became less a nation of rooted institutions and more a place of rootless individuals. And so I grieved for my departing country too.

But maybe all losses are no more than personal. Sometimes individuals lose, and societies gain. Maybe someone's loss of privilege is another's gain in dignity. Perhaps there is a selfishness to every song of lament.

I doubt I will ever cease to reflect. When I've tried to despise the Sixties, I've never quite been able to. The rebels of that decade got two things supremely right. They saw the civil rights revolution as long overdue and the Vietnam War as a tragic mistake. More than that, they saw America had been too busy growing, achieving, and flexing its muscle to be sensitive to the sheer miseries the human condition can create.

What was good about the 1960s—and there was good—came at so heavy a cost that it became impossible to discern what tradition, institution, or belief the disillusioned did not want to desecrate. You can't build a nation on nihilism: it takes vision and values to do that.

What values? Family, church, school, country? Abiding words had altered meanings. The Sixties left no star to steer by. Once I thought myself alone in being stranded in the middle of a great, vast sea. Until I raised my eyes and saw a million rudderless boats like me.

The debates engendered during the Sixties will probably persist in one form or another as long as America claims nationhood. The values stolen were not the property of any race or party or philosophy or creed. They reside rather at the heart of human nature and at the core of nationhood as well. Without them we today lack personal or national identity, and that's what makes our boats drifting in the Sixties' wake so sad.

When one speaks of the Greatest Generation, ours will never come to mind. Yet from the fires of destruction can come shoots of rebirth. Democracy and law, freedom and enterprise—these can be, if we make them, triumphs of humanity as well as towers of strength. But that achievement too requires that America not remain the Sixties' land of disbelief.

It may be too much to hope that the decade that still tears us apart may play some role in bringing us together. The shared memory of the Civil War in time made us a stronger country, but only after Grant and Lee sat down in that plain room at Appomattox could the long healing process even begin.

There has been no truce, no surrender in the war of the Sixties. The polarization has deepened as we have migrated to places with "people like ourselves." Yet as the generation that lived through those years passes along, it may be more possible to lay down arms and assess what that crucial time gave us and what it took away. In my own mind, the damage to this nation has been enormous, but those who see the decade differently have strong points to make as well. Perhaps we can work to recover from the bad and continue to build upon the good. Perhaps, for the sake of America, we can by the end of life become friends too.

Those who love history also understand its relevance, even when that relevance is difficult to pinpoint or define. With the study of history comes an appreciation of the multiplicity of causes, the inevitability of change, the irreversibility of time. The Sixties were not the sole cause of anything—few things ever are—but they were a powerful contributor to our present ailments, and I hope what we have lost won't leave our descendants lonely in the woods. It is their destiny, not ours, but it is our duty to show that there are deep, abiding constants in this world, if one can but discover them, and that one may just find them in the values the Sixties stole away. In those values lie purpose and a compass, and the hope that generations to come will find their way.

As a robin's breast turns golden in deep sunset, so my reflections on the Sixties now assume an olden hue. We're a beautiful country, the best that ever was, but the Sixties left us much work to do. That the decade opened opportunity to millions there can be no doubt. But at what cost? What war does to our lives, what depression does to our livelihoods, that decade did to our spirits. In shattered values and beliefs, in weakened communities and discredited institutions, those years often shut off opportunity to Americans who needed it most. It is not too much to ask that we acknowledge all we have lost and what we must yet find. We came close to losing our wonderful country in the 1960s, and that must never happen again. America must not become one more fallen faith.

Acknowledgments

One may conceive of a book almost as a lengthy letter. The writer sits down at his desk and proceeds more or less straight through to a sign-off.

That is not how this book unfolded. It began as jottings more than fifty years ago and expanded here and there over the next half-century. Much of it recalls conversations and happenings many decades back, and I have tried as best I can to guard against the tricks of memory.

A memoir is by definition a recollection of the past, but the past does not yield clarity quickly. It becomes more meaningful when placed in the context of present and future, so it seemed essential to ask what bearing the 1950s and '60s have on our world today. Memoirs and social commentary are often thought of as distinct genres, but the strengths of each form of expression are sometimes better blended.

To do this, I have required a great deal of help from many people over many years. Much of that help was rendered inadvertently by those I met along life's way. I do thank them for the part they played in shaping my experience and understanding. I refer to them in the book by first name only, and indeed I have changed those names to protect their privacy.

My longtime friend Barbara Perry, of the Miller Center at the University of Virginia, has often lifted my flagging spirits with her faith in this endeavor. And University of Virginia Professor Laurens Walker is the best sounding board any writer could have.

What a delight it has been to work with the good folks at Encounter Books. Roger Kimball's writing has always expanded my horizons, and it has been an honor to work with him and his cheerful and dedicated team. They have made the publishing process a pleasure from beginning to end.

It was my stroke of good fortune to have such a fine literary agent as Glen Hartley of Writers' Representatives. Glen brings to the task superb literary judgment, business acumen, and the caring insight of a friend.

An early version of Chapter 3 was published as "Will Law Survive the 1960s?" in *The Green Bag, An Entertaining Journal of Law* (vol. 11, 2007). The esteemed editor of that journal, Professor Ross Davies of George Mason University, has my thanks for all his good support.

Part of the dedication of this book, "To My Beloved Country," acknowledges a debt to Alan Paton's beautiful and poignant novel, *Cry, the Beloved Country*. The fabric of his country and mine has been terribly torn. In that sadness lies the hope that a generation that rends a garment may yet help to mend it, while and if there is still time.

When public events become discouraging, one repairs to the personal. In that respect, I have been lucky. My dear wife, Lossie, has always been there for me. This book is dedicated first and foremost to her, the great love of my life.

Index